Recipes for Learning

Recipes for Learning

Exploring the Curriculum Through Cooking

GAIL LEWIS

JEAN M. SHAW

Library of Congress Cataloging in Publication Data

Lewis, Gail.
    Recipes for learning.

    1. Cookery—Study and teaching. I. Shaw, Jean M.,
joint author. II. Title
TX661.L48   641.5   79-338
ISBN 0-87620-803-0

Current Printing (last number):

10 9 8 7 6 5 4 3 2 1

Y-8030-2

Book and cover design by **Karen McBride**
Illustrated by **Karen McBride** and **Susan Cuscuna**

Contents

Recipes at a Glance

Recipe	Appliance no cook	Appliance small appliance	Appliance oven	Food Group Milk, Protein	Food Group Fat	Food Group Fruits Vegetables	Food Group Bread	Cost Low	Cost Moderate	Subject Matter Art	Subject Matter Language	Subject Matter Math	Subject Matter Science	Subject Matter Other
Butter	•			•	•			•		•	•	•	•	field trips
Celery, Carrot	•					•			•	•	•	•	•	game
Dil Dip	•			•	•				•	•	•	•	•	
Design A Drink	•					•			•	•	•	•		
Fruit Fun	•					•				•	•	•	•	game
Peanut Butter Candy	•			•	•			•		•	•	•	•	game
Soap Sculpture	•							•		•	•	•	•	
Applesauce		hot plate				•		•	•	•	•	•	•	self-concept, game
Carob Candy		hot plate			•	•			•	•	•	•	•	puppet
Finger Jell-O		hot plate				•		•		•	•	•	•	creative movement
Finger Paint		hot plate						•		•	•	•		game
Pancakes		fry pan					•	•		•	•	•	•	
Play Dough		hot plate						•	•	•	•	•	•	play dough cards
Popcorn		popper					•	•		•	•	•	•	creative movement
Vegetable Stew		crock pot				•			•	•	•	•	•	song
Granola			•	•	•				•	•	•	•	•	
Pretzels			•				•	•		•	•	•		game
Shrink-A-Shape			•					•		•	•	•		
Sourdough Bread			•				•	•		•	•	•	•	game

From *Recipes for Learning* by Gail Lewis and Jean M. Shaw, ©1979 by Goodyear Publishing Company, Inc.

CHAPTER ONE

Introduction:
The Joy of
Classroom Cooking

A world of fun and learning awaits the children and teachers who use the recipes and activities in this book. A wide variety of cooking methods and procedures are presented, including no-cook, hot plate, small-appliance, and oven recipes. *Recipes for Learning* also includes foods from all groups, recipes in both standard and metric measurements, and a balance of food and art recipes.

Following each recipe are teacher cards and children's cards featuring related explorations that can be done before and after cooking as well as during recipe preparation. Also offered are reproducible pages for take-home recipes and for class worksheets, games, and cutouts as well as a chart indicating the specific skills and features of each recipe. These reproducible pages may be adapted to other pages in the book. *Recipes for Learning* also includes general suggestions for planning, financing, and carrying out cooking activities, information on the skills and values of cooking, and a guide to metric measurements.

SKILLS AND VALUES ACQUIRED THROUGH COOKING

Most children like to eat, and cooking what they eat is even more fun. Cooking is a "grown-up" thing to do, and many children have had little experience with it. Even children who have had previous cooking experience at home or in school will enjoy and learn from these cooking activities. Preparing food and art materials provides opportunities for active involvement and lets the children use all their senses. For these reasons, cooking is an exciting, motivating, valid classroom experience.

3

A planned program of cooking in the classroom is a good vehicle for exploring, reinforcing, and supplementing the curriculum. Many skills, concepts, and values can be introduced and practiced by the teacher who plans cooking activities well and capitalizes on the many learning opportunities they provide. Following are some examples of specific areas in which cooking projects can help reinforce learning:

Math   Telling time; recognizing numerals; measuring and weighing; using ordinal numbers; counting skills; estimating; using mathematics in a practical way.

Science   Origins of foods; nutritional values of foods; predicting, hypothesizing, and generalizing; sensory experiences; observing physical properties and changes.

Reading and language   Left-to-right tracking; sequencing; oral expression; vocabulary development; auditory discrimination; sight vocabulary.

Cultural development   New art processes with cooking ingredients; creative-movement exercises; customs related to foods; stories, poems, and jokes.

Some of the related projects and activities are:
- Science activities and sensory explorations related to the foods prepared.
- Math activities that emphasize counting, computing, measuring, and data-recording skills.
- Language-arts activities that help children develop prereading and reading skills as well as skills in listening, speaking, and writing.
- Opportunities for social development through dramatic play and planned social experiences.
- Creative art ideas.
- Poetry, literature, and song cards to accompany cooking experiences.
- Bulletin board ideas.
- Teacher cards giving background information, teaching tips, and shopping and equipment lists.
- Games designed to reinforce learning while having fun.

Such a list can be expanded as the needs of children dictate. Exploring many curricular areas around one central theme adds unity and reality to classroom experiences. This type of planning also challenges teachers to develop new approaches to their usual routine, which can be stimulating and exciting.

Through cooking experiences, children have the opportunity to plan, share, cooperate, and learn together. They may form better habits of eating, because they will discover that nutritious foods can also taste good—and they can be introduced to new foods or new ways of preparing them in the classroom. Cooking in a group also encourages informal conversation and exchange of observations, which can generate enthusiasm and ideas to pursue in more formal discussion sessions.

SUGGESTIONS FOR USING THE BOOK

The recipes can either be reproduced or actually removed from the book for use during each cooking activity. Each recipe can be slipped into a clear plastic folder, covered with clear contact paper, or laminated so that it can be used many times without being torn or soiled. Recipes could be stored with teacher cards, children cards, worksheets, and other related activities for that specific recipe or they can all be kept together in ring binders to make a recipe book for the cooking center.

The teacher cards are printed four to a page (front and back). These pages may be removed from the book or they may be reproduced; then the cards can be cut apart and stored in a 3-by-5-inch file box. These cards may also be laminated for protection.

The children's cards can be removed from the book (or reproduced), cut apart, and filed in a folder or box at the cooking center. Again, they may be covered in plastic or laminated so that they will last.

The worksheets and activities in Chapter 7 can be reproduced for the children to use with the corresponding cooking projects. These activities are either self-explanatory or are explained on a teacher card.

SUGGESTIONS FOR USING EACH RECIPE SECTION

1. Read the recipe and the suggested activities on teacher cards, children cards, and related worksheets.
2. Choose those activities suitable for your particular group of children and make any necessary adaptations or changes.
3. Schedule the cooking experience. Plan times for related activities before, during, or after the recipe is made.
4. Shop, set up, cook, clean up . . . eat (or with the non-edible recipes, use the materials the children have cooked up).
5. File the cards and recipes after using them. Add your own teaching suggestions to the file and make notes about changes or improvements in the recipes or procedures.
6. Choose another recipe and repeat the cycle.

THE COOKING CENTER

A cooking center, like any interest center, is a place where materials, equipment, and activities relating to that center are kept. A center should contain activities to introduce, reinforce, enrich, and relate to many different developmental levels so that any child can find something to do. You may wish to keep recipe books, equipment, children's cards, worksheets, and staple ingredients in your cooking center, as well as activities related to the recipe you are concentrating on. The center could be a special table, shelf, counter top, or several boxes assembled together.

You may not want to set up a cooking center; although a special place in the room is nice, it isn't essential. You need to think about the available space, the frequency of cooking activities, and your own preferences. The important thing is to experience cooking with your children and see how much learning can take place.

USING METRIC MEASUREMENTS WITH RECIPES

American educators differ on when and how the metric system should be taught to young children, but most agree that it must be taught. Learning new information is most meaningful to children if it can be applied in a real situation, and using metric measurements of volume, weight, and length in cooking is an excellent introduction. For that reason, the recipes in this book are printed twice—first with metric, and then with standard, measures. For effective exposure to the metric system, use the metric recipe; for more practice with standard measures, use the standard recipe.

When a child sees that a popcorn popper holds 3 liters of popped corn, that a banana is 25 centimeters long, or that the flour needed to make twenty pancakes weighs 150 grams, these terms take on meaning and are less likely to be forgotten or confused. When they work with actual ingredients and real measuring tools, children discover that learning to measure is important, and they are highly motivated to be accurate in their measurements because they want the recipe to "turn out right."

The great majority of measures in recipes are measures of volume—that is, liters and milliliters replace quarts, pints, cups, tablespoons, and teaspoons. Metric measures of weight can also be explored in cooking experiences, as most food packages are marked in both standard (pounds and ounces) and metric (grams and kilograms) weights. Before the ingredients are removed, have the children hold packages or cans to see if they feel "heavy," "light," or "in between," and have them weigh the packages to confirm the weights. Actually feeling and holding a 500-gram weight (a little over a pound) helps make the terms and numbers meaningful.

Teachers may also want to let children hold various ingredients, guess their weight, and then confirm their guesses by weighing the ingredients. This guess-and-check or estimate-and-confirm method lets children use their own reasoning powers to deal with real measuring problems. Many children improve rapidly in their ability to estimate while others make slower progress, but they all see meaning in numbers and measurements when they actually handle objects and measuring tools.

Measures of length—centimeters and millimeters—can also be used to a limited extent in recipe preparation. For example, the children can estimate and confirm the length and circumference of fruits and vegetables to be used in a recipe. Even the circumference of popcorn—unpopped, then popped—can be measured. If ingredients come in boxes or trays, these containers can be measured, as can pancakes, play-dough creations, loaves of bread, and pretzels. Older children can calculate the volume of containers and then express the volume in cubic centimeters or millimeters. Once the metric tape measure or ruler has found its way into the cooking area, the youngsters themselves will suggest many ways to use it.

Specific measuring activities are included with every recipe in this book. Teachers will find many ways to expand and vary these experiences. If you use your own recipes, you may want to convert the measurements to metrics before presenting them to the children. Following are the approximate conversions for changing standard to metric measurements.

Standard	Metric
1 quart	1 liter or 1000 milliliters
1 pint	½ liter or 500 milliliters
1 cup	¼ liter or 250 milliliters
½ cup	125 milliliters
¼ cup	60 milliliters
1 tablespoon	15 milliliters

1 teaspoon	5 milliliters
½ teaspoon	2½ milliliters
¼ teaspoon	1¼ milliliters

Although these conversions are not exact (1 cup actually equals 242 milliliters, for example), metric measuring cups are clearly marked with the units shown above, and, therefore, the correct amounts are easy for children to see and use.

Most variety and hardware stores now stock glass and metal measuring cups marked with both standard and metric measurements. Large department stores and science-supply houses also have a wide variety of measuring tools. Measuring spoons may not be so easy to find, but with a permanent felt-tip pen you can mark the handles of ordinary measuring spoons with their metric equivalents.

These words—do, participate, estimate, measure, use—are the keys to successful mastery of common metric measurements. Practical experience will help children (and adults) learn metrics in a meaningful way, and preparing recipes is a good method of providing this experience—so use, use, use the metric recipes.

ABBREVIATIONS USED IN THE BOOK

Following is a list of the abbreviations used in the recipes and activities. You may wish to make a chart of these for the children to refer to when you begin your cooking activities.

Standard	Metric
c. — cup	g — gram
T. — tablespoon	mg — milligram
t. — teaspoon	l — liter
lb. — pound	ml — milliliter
oz. — ounce	cm — centimeter
in. — inch	mm — millimeter
F. — Fahrenheit scale	C — Celsius scale

CHAPTER
TWO

Getting Ready to Cook

CAREFUL PLANNING EQUALS MORE LEARNING

Careful planning provides for good use of time and prepares both the teacher and children to take full advantage of the learning opportunities that are possible with cooking experiences. These five steps are suggested:

1. Select a recipe
   - Be sure the recipe suits the level of the children. It should be easy for them to do yet provide a challenge or two. Perhaps it will introduce a new word or concept, or help in the development of a small-muscle skill.
   - Be sure there is enough for a small group to do—break the recipe into parts so that each child can do one or two steps. If necessary to give more turns, flour can be sifted twice or two different chaildren can measure two cups of sugar.
   - When possible, have the children cut or garnish their own serving and form their own cookies, candies, popcorn balls, or pretzels.
2. Do research and gather resource materials
   - Find out about ingredients—how and where do they grow? How are they processed? Are certain foods associated with special uses, traditions, or customs?
   - Be sure to find science activities to complement the recipe's directions. Observing, classifying, comparing, measuring, dissolving, grinding, and crushing can be done. Some ingredients can be grown. Be sure to include many sensory explorations.
   - Find related books, pictures, films, filmstrips, songs, fingerplays, and poems.

3. Gather materials and equipment
   - Plan ahead to make sure you have everything you need for each recipe.
   - Use lists to check equipment and ingredients. Older children can help.
   - With some recipes, an adult should plan to stay with the group once cooking has begun.
   - Gather tasting spoons or sticks.
   - Gather napkins, spoons, and plates for eating, if necessary.
4. Cooking time!
   - Cooking is a small-group activity—use a chart to help children take turns, and let everyone sample as you cook.
   - In some cases, each child can make his or her own piece of candy, pretzel, or pancake from a recipe made by the small group.
   - Take time to measure carefully—make it a learning experience.
   - Pass the bowl or pan around the group when mixing or adding ingredients so that everyone has a turn.
   - Taste the ingredients as you work. Sample small portions with toothpicks, plastic spoons, popsicle sticks, wooden coffee stirrers, tongue depressors, or even small pieces of clean paper.
   - Put used utensils aside, perhaps in a dish pan.
   - Review steps and procedures in sequence.
   - Make plans for eating and sharing the food.
5. Cleanup time is part of the process
   - Allot sufficient time to clean utensils and cooking area before eating.
   - Take turns on cleanup duty.
   - Wrap garbage—perhaps some of it can be used as pet food or put in a compost heap.
   - Wipe stove or hotplate.
   - Return equipment.
   - Write thank-you notes if ingredients or utensils have been supplied by parents or if someone outside the class has helped in any way.

PAYING FOR COOKING ACTIVITIES

Naturally, cooking in the classroom costs money, but there are many ways to finance your cooking projects. For example:

- Regular school budget or direct tuition. A dollar per child per semester—less than most workbooks—would allow a class to cook many times.
- Contributions from the children—25 cents a month or 10 cents a week for example. If the children normally buy snacks, they might want to contribute some of their snack money to cooking activities occasionally.
- Each parent can donate a staple or an ingredient for one recipe.
- A civic club or senior citizens' group might want to have a service project to support cooking in the school.
- Teacher "treat"—you can occasionally bring popcorn or cocoa and sugar; the children could use milk they have bought at school to make hot chocolate.

SHOPPING FOR SUPPLIES

Bringing in the groceries is work that can be shared. For example:

- School secretary, aide, or teachers can take turns.
- Parents or room mothers might be willing to help with shopping.
- PTA or service committee could be asked to shop for classes.
- Shop for staples and other ingredients on a field trip to a supermarket.

HEALTH AND SAFETY PROCEDURES

Several safety measures are necessary to ensure smooth, safely run cooking experiences.

- Find out if any of the children are allergic to any foods you plan to use or if any of the foods must be restricted in their diets. Keep this information handy for reference.
- Make sure the children have clean hands before cooking begins. Wash in the restroom, bring damp cloths to the table, or use packaged premoistened towels.
- Explain why it is important to taste only from one's own spoon or stick.
- Roll up the children's sleeves so they won't get burned, messy, or wet.
- Set up the hot plate near the teacher, if possible. Turn the handles of pots and pans so that the children won't bump into them. Tape down any extension cords so children won't trip over them. Be sure the hot plate or toaster oven is stable and secure so that it won't wobble.
- Keep a jar of salt or soda nearby to smother any fires that might occur.
- Treat burns with cold water.
- Use an asbestos pad under the hot plate.
- Use knives only on cutting boards or several layers of paper towels. Stress the idea that knives should be used down low—not waved in the air.
- Keep plenty of dry potholders handy.
- Have a damp sponge or paper towels to wipe up spills.

TOPICS FOR YOUNG COOKS TO DISCUSS

During pauses in recipe procedures, while waiting for something to cook, or as you eat, many related topics can profitably be discussed. Some conversation starters are:

- Other recipes that use some of the same ingredients or procedures.
- Information on food labels.
- Shapes and sizes of containers—rectangles, circles, ovals, and squares can all be found on boxes and cans. Discuss also the materials of the containers—paper, cardboard, plastic, metals, and others can be found.
- Children's cooking experiences: Do they cook at home or at a relative's or friend's house? Who does cook at home? Who shops? When? How?
- The cost of foods may be classified as expensive, reasonable, or cheap. Where are the prices marked? What does "2 for 59¢" mean? What foods are sold by the pound, piece, box, can, liter, gram, etc.?

- How can foods be classified? Suggest different ways, such as:

    Food groups—meats, dairy products, breads and cereals, fruits and vegetables.

    Foods that are eaten raw, foods that are always cooked, foods that may be eaten both ways.

    Foods that are eaten hot, those that are eaten cold.

    Greasy vs. not greasy foods.

    Textures of foods—crisp vs. "gooey," wet vs. dry, etc.

    Colors of foods.

    Time of day foods are usually eaten—breakfast, lunch, dinner, between meals.

    Processed vs. unprocessed foods.

    Changes of states in matter—solids, liquids, gases.

    Senses that are used in food preparation—all senses are used in most recipes.

- Each recipe will have its own vocabulary to work on. What words are new? What do they mean? What words describe the ingredients or finished products for each recipe? What do the abbreviations stand for?
- Where are foods grown? How? When?
- What else could the ingredients be used for?

CHAPTER
THREE

No-Cook Recipes

Homemade Butter

Pour 60 ml whipping cream into each of 4 baby-food jars. Add a few grains salt and 1 drop yellow food coloring to each jar. Tightly close each jar. Now shake. Butter will form after several minutes. Pour off any liquid. Serve immediately, or chill and then serve.

From *Recipes for Learning* by Gail Lewis and Jean M. Shaw, ©1979 by Goodyear Publishing Company, Inc.

Homemade Butter

Pour ¼ cup whipping cream into each of 4 baby-food jars. Add a few grains salt and 1 drop food coloring to each jar. Tightly close each jar. Now shake. Butter will form after several minutes. Pour off any liquid. Serve immediately, or chill and then serve.

From *Recipes for Learning* by Gail Lewis and Jean M. Shaw, ©1979 by Goodyear Publishing Company, Inc.

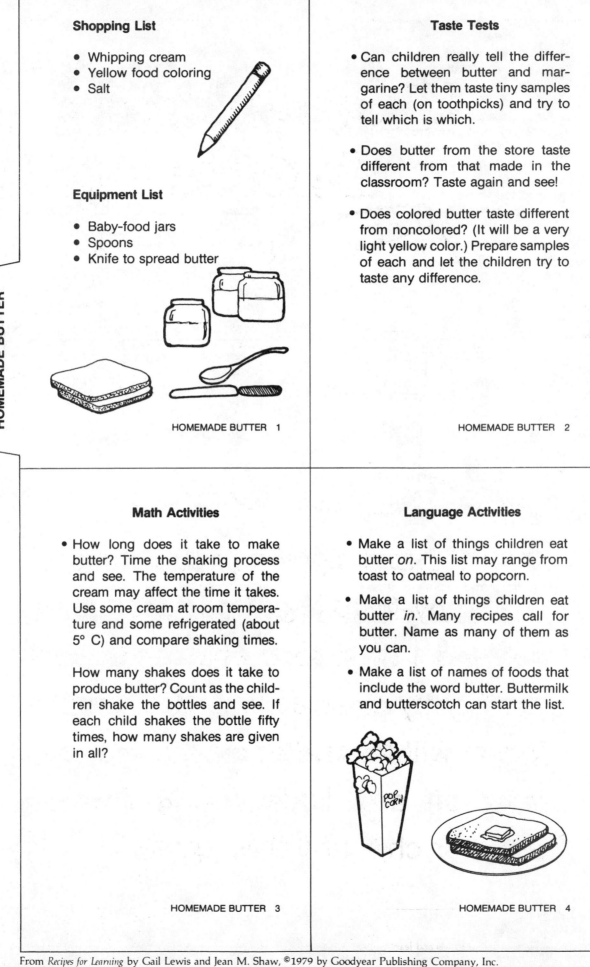

Shopping List

- Whipping cream
- Yellow food coloring
- Salt

Equipment List

- Baby-food jars
- Spoons
- Knife to spread butter

HOMEMADE BUTTER

Taste Tests

- Can children really tell the difference between butter and margarine? Let them taste tiny samples of each (on toothpicks) and try to tell which is which.

- Does butter from the store taste different from that made in the classroom? Taste again and see!

- Does colored butter taste different from noncolored? (It will be a very light yellow color.) Prepare samples of each and let the children try to taste any difference.

Math Activities

- How long does it take to make butter? Time the shaking process and see. The temperature of the cream may affect the time it takes. Use some cream at room temperature and some refrigerated (about 5° C) and compare shaking times.

  How many shakes does it take to produce butter? Count as the children shake the bottles and see. If each child shakes the bottle fifty times, how many shakes are given in all?

Language Activities

- Make a list of things children eat butter *on*. This list may range from toast to oatmeal to popcorn.

- Make a list of things children eat butter *in*. Many recipes call for butter. Name as many of them as you can.

- Make a list of names of foods that include the word butter. Buttermilk and butterscotch can start the list.

More Taste Tests

- Why is salt added to butter? Taste salted and nonsalted butter and see which the children prefer.

- What does goat's-milk butter taste like? Try to obtain cream from a goat or other animal, and compare its taste with cow's-cream butter.

- Taste the watery liquid that is left after the butter is made. Does it taste like buttermilk? What differences in appearance can the children notice?

Food Colors

Butter is yellow, bread is white or brown, strawberries are red. Work with children to extend the list. You might include multicolored foods. Cut pictures from magazines. Make large posters or pictures to brighten up your room.

Red Foods
strawberries
catsup
spaghetti sauce

Green Foods
beans
lettuce
spinach

Yellow Foods
squash
corn
butter

More Language Activities

- Make all the words you can from the letters in HOMEMADE BUTTER.

- Investigate the origin and meaning of "buttery" phrases such as buttering up, bread and butter (used as meaning money), buttercup, or butter fingers.

- Make up some new "butter" words and invent meanings for them.

More Math Activities

- How many milliliters are there in a drop of food color? Chances are, not even one! Try to measure the *fraction* of a milliliter in a drop of food color; you may be able to borrow a druggist's or chemist's tool to do so.

- How much watery liquid is left in each jar after the butter is formed? Carefully pour it off and measure the liquid from each jar in milliliters. Was more liquid formed in one jar than in another?

18

From *Recipes for Learning* by Gail Lewis and Jean M. Shaw, ©1979 by Goodyear Publishing Company, Inc.

Visit a Dairy

Form committees to plan a trip to a dairy. You might form some of the following groups.

- Transportation
- Questions
- Research
- Thank you

After your visit, summarize information you obtained in some of these ways:

- Written report
- Mural
- TV news show
- Booklet for a younger class

Shapes for Butter

Borrow butter molds. Perhaps a parent or grandparent can lend you some. Use the molds to make different shapes for butter.

Cut butter curls. Make sure the butter is very cold. Run a vegetable peeler over it to make a very thin, curly shape.

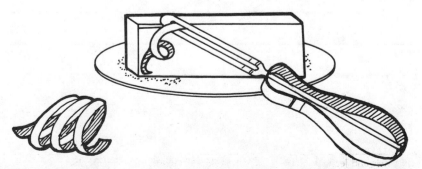

19

From *Recipes for Learning* by Gail Lewis and Jean M. Shaw, ©1979 by Goodyear Publishing Company, Inc.

Butter Churning

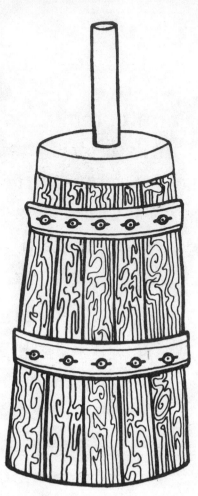

Find a way to observe butter churning. Perhaps you could visit an older person who makes his own butter, or maybe a farmer or Home Economics Extension worker could visit your class to show how to churn butter. If possible, try to help with butter churning.

Butter, Butter, and More Butter!

What can you use butter for? Make your favorite recipe at home or school, and enjoy fresh homemade butter on it. List as many dishes or recipes as you can that use butter.

_____

_____

_____

_____

_____

From _Recipes for Learning_ by Gail Lewis and Jean M. Shaw, ©1979 by Goodyear Publishing Company, Inc.

Carrot & Celery Snacks

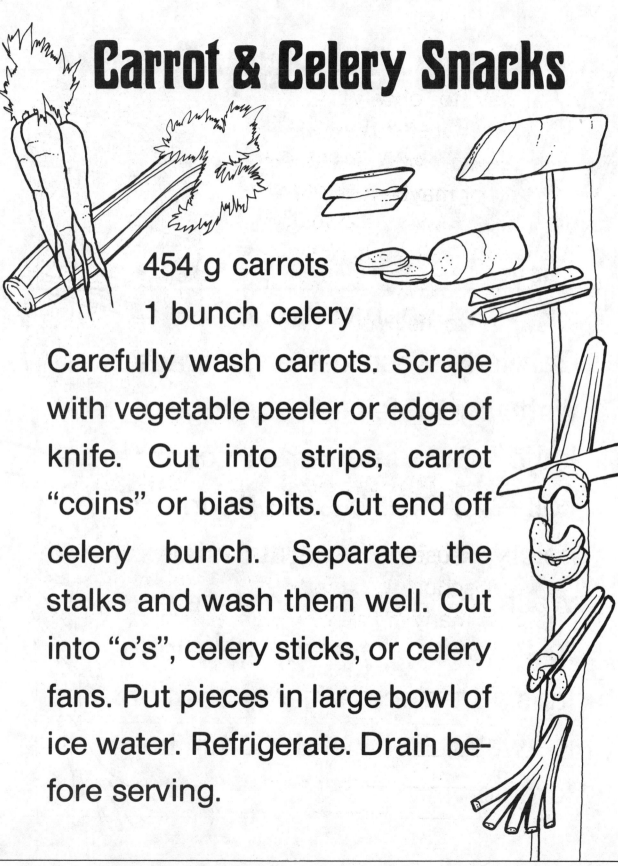

454 g carrots

1 bunch celery

Carefully wash carrots. Scrape with vegetable peeler or edge of knife. Cut into strips, carrot "coins" or bias bits. Cut end off celery bunch. Separate the stalks and wash them well. Cut into "c's", celery sticks, or celery fans. Put pieces in large bowl of ice water. Refrigerate. Drain before serving.

From *Recipes for Learning* by Gail Lewis and Jean M. Shaw, ©1979 by Goodyear Publishing Company, Inc.

Carrot & Celery Snacks

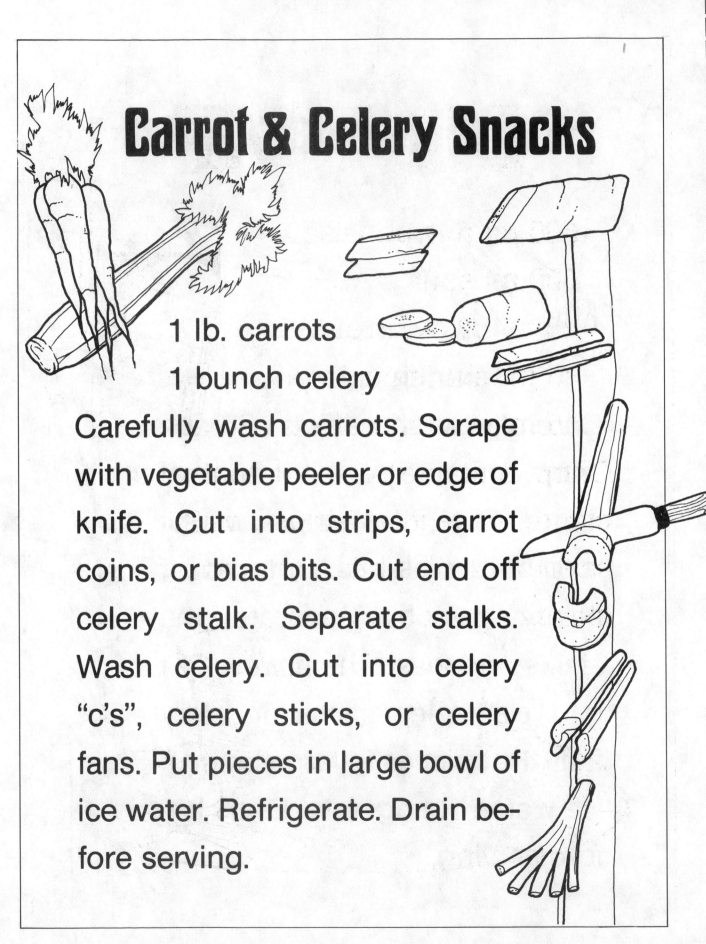

1 lb. carrots

1 bunch celery

Carefully wash carrots. Scrape with vegetable peeler or edge of knife. Cut into strips, carrot coins, or bias bits. Cut end off celery stalk. Separate stalks. Wash celery. Cut into celery "c's", celery sticks, or celery fans. Put pieces in large bowl of ice water. Refrigerate. Drain before serving.

From *Recipes for Learning* by Gail Lewis and Jean M. Shaw, ©1979 by Goodyear Publishing Company, Inc.

DILL DIP

500 ml mayonnaise

500 ml sour cream

45 ml dill weed

45 ml chopped onion

15 ml seasoned salt

Chop onion. Put mayonnaise, sour cream, dill, and salt in a bowl. Stir. Use as dip for vegetables, crackers, or chips.

From *Recipes for Learning* by Gail Lewis and Jean M. Shaw, ©1979 by Goodyear Publishing Company, Inc.

DILL DIP

2 c. mayonnaise

2 c. sour cream

3 T. dill weed

3 T. chopped onion

1 T. seasoned salt

Chop onion. Put mayonnaise, sour cream, dill and salt in a bowl. Stir. Use as dip for vegetables, crackers, or chips.

24

Shopping List

- Carrots
- Celery
- Mayonnaise
- Sour cream
- Dill weed
- Onion
- Seasoned salt

Equipment List

- Table knives
- Cutting board or paper towels
- Large bowl
- Mixing bowl, spoons
- Measuring cup, spoons
- Knife
- Vegetable peeler

CARROT AND CELERY SNACKS 5

Language Activities

- Alike and Different . . .
Examine carrot and celery sticks (look at them, smell, taste, feel them, break them in two and hear the crunch, eat them and listen to the sound.) Now discuss and list as many ways as you can that carrots and celery are alike and different. Try the same for mayonnaise and sour cream.

- Dippers . . .
Carrot and celery sticks can be used as dippers. They are crunchy and they are long and slim ("slimmos"). Talk about other foods or objects that have these same characteristics or some of them—the list may range from crackers to green beans.

CARROT AND CELERY SNACKS 6

How Big Around?

Is the circumference of a carrot bigger or smaller than a child's thumb? By how much? Compare the measurements of each by wrapping yarn around them. Now lay the string out along a ruler and see how many centimeters long it is. Let the children suggest other circumferences to measure and compare. Always predict measurements first, then verify.

CARROT AND CELERY SNACKS 7

Carrot-Print Stationery

Let the children make stationery with small carrot prints. Cut a design into the end of a stub of carrot. Dip into a small amount of tempera paint. Carefully print onto paper. Make envelopes to match. An easy pattern:

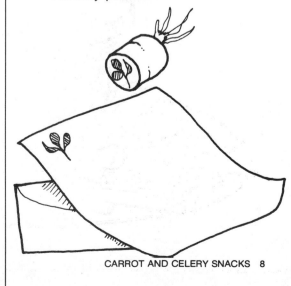

CARROT AND CELERY SNACKS 8

25

From *Recipes for Learning* by Gail Lewis and Jean M. Shaw, ©1979 by Goodyear Publishing Company, Inc.

Carrot and Celery Words

Pronounce words that begin with hard and soft c and classify them according to beginning sound as "carrot" or "celery" words. Use word cards. Let the children sort them according to hard c or soft c sound. Suggestions:

Hard C

carrot	cabbage	car
cantaloupe	caboose	cake
carpet	cabin	camel
coin	cab	can

Soft C

city	cinnamon	ceiling
circus	cymbal	citizen
cell	cider	Cinderella
circle	cigarette	cylinder

Make up sentences that include both hard c and soft c words. For example, Cecil carried cider to the city.

Observations

Talk to the children as they work. Many things can be explored:

- Carrots have crosswise rings but celery has lengthwise ribs.
- Celery ribs may be peeled off. They are stringy.
- Celery leaves are a deeper color than the stalks. Inner stalks are usually paler in color than outside stalks.
- Mayonnaise and sour cream have a few differences when examined closely:
  color—smell—the way they "pour" —taste
- Many types of onion are available— fresh (Bermuda, yellow, white, red), frozen, dried, scallions, shallots. These all look, taste, and smell different. Examine several kinds if possible.
- Examine and smell celery seeds and compare to fresh celery.

Carrot-Print Math

Let the children use the carrot printers from the stationery activity for a math experience. Write a math fact (addition or multiplication) and then "illustrate" it with carrot prints. Write in answer or "print a fact;" then write in the problem.

$$3 + 4 =$$

$$5 \times 2 =$$

More Measurements

- Arrange all the carrots from the bunch in order, from smallest to largest. Measure the length of each and record it.

- Now arrange each stalk of celery in order, from smallest to largest. Measure the length of each stalk and record it.

- Compare the number of carrots and the number of celery stalks. Now compare the longest carrot to the longest celery stalk. How many centimeters longer is one than the other? Compare the shortest carrot to the shortest celery stalk. How many centimeters longer is one than the other?

From *Recipes for Learning* by Gail Lewis and Jean M. Shaw, ©1979 by Goodyear Publishing Company, Inc.

Brightly colored **carrots** are famous for being rich in vitamin A, which prevents night blindness. Their carotene is used for coloring and enriching margarine and dairy products. Carrots have been grown by men for at least 2000 years; they were developed from wild carrots in Europe and Asia. In the United States, carrots are grown widely; Texas, California, and Arizona farmers produce the most carrots. People enjoy eating carrots raw or cooked, and they are also fed to stock animals. Carrots are planted in early spring and take sixty to ninety days to mature. Well known as a diet food, **celery** is very low in calories. It is very "crunchy" and provides plenty of chewing practice when eaten raw. Celery is a relatively poor source of vitamins and minerals, but it provides necessary roughage in the diet. Both the stalks and the leaves of celery can be eaten raw or cooked. The seed of celery plants, which is produced every two years, is dried and sold as a spice or seasoning. Celery is grown in many areas of the United States; California, Florida, and Michigan produce the most celery. Farmers sometimes must protect celery plants from the sun to maintain their pale green color. Cardboard, plastic, or wood planks are used to cover the plants. Celery is best grown in loamy soil in mild temperatures. Find out more about carrots and celery.

Meet the Stars of the Snack Show

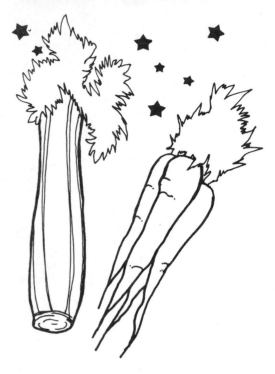

Science . . . Growing Carrots

Carrots can be easily grown from tops of carrots. Cut off an inch or two from the top of each carrot. Place in a shallow dish of water. Add gravel if desired. Change water twice a week. Roots will grow. Plant in dirt when roots are well formed.

27

List-a-Word

Make as many words as you can from the letters in
CARROT — CELERY — DILL DIP
List the words. Compare lists with a friend. Some starters:

car
deep
rot
road
lip
rid
cell
dear

Science . . .

Plant Circulatory System

See how water and nutrients travel in the "veins" of plants. Put several drops of food color in a glass of water and place a stalk of celery in the glass. In an hour, color will be visible in the leaves. Cut the celery and see the color in the veins.

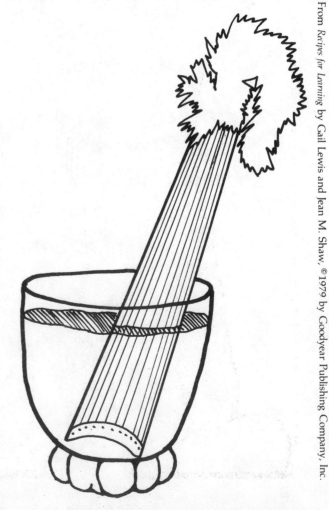

28

From *Recipes for Learning* by Gail Lewis and Jean M. Shaw. ©1979 by Goodyear Publishing Company, Inc.

Design-a-Drink

Provide various juices and mixers such as gingerale, 7-Up, Sprite, club soda, etc. for each child. Have either metric or standard (or both) measuring spoons and cups available. Each child should write down his or her recipe as it is mixed in a cup. These recipes can be exchanged so that the children can try each others' recipes.

Equipment List

- Paper cups
- Measuring cups and spoons
- Index cards or paper
- Plastic Spoons

Shopping List

Juices and soft drinks

Suggestions

This recipe is best done in small groups or individually. The ingredients and equipment could be set up on a table to be used during a free-choice period. Index cards and paper should be available so that the children can record their recipes as they "design a drink."

DESIGN-A-DRINK   9

Design-a-Glass

Give each child a clear plastic disposable glass. The children can design the glasses they use for their drinks by using permanent felt-tip markers. These can be washed after using and taken home.

DESIGN-A-DRINK   10

"Design a Drink" Cookbook

- Let each child copy his or her drink recipe on a spirit master. These can be run off and put together as a cookbook to take home. The children can add illustrations and make a cover out of construction paper.

- Let each child think of a name for his or her drink.
  Examples: Jean's Juice
  Carl's Cooler

DESIGN-A-DRINK   11

Enlarge the Recipe

Let each child take a recipe and change it so that it would make enough for two, five or ten people—or the whole class. The children could work in pairs to check each other's computations.

DESIGN-A-DRINK   12

31

From *Recipes for Learning* by Gail Lewis and Jean M. Shaw, ©1979 by Goodyear Publishing Company, Inc.

Classifying Activity

Use the worksheet in Chapter 7 (page 171) with the pictures of two glasses for one of the following activities. Children will need scissors, glue, and old magazines or newspapers. Let them cut out and classify by gluing pictures or words in the glasses. The following are some ways to classify pictures or words:

1. Things I like to drink—Things I don't like to drink
2. Foods—Drinks
3. Drinks that are good for me— Drinks that are bad for me
4. Liquids I can drink—Liquids I can't drink

More Suggestions

Design-a-drink could be done as a culminating activity for a unit on liquid measurements they will be using. The children could share in the expense of the ingredients by contributing the price of a soft drink or by bringing one ingredient—for example, one kind of juice, one soft drink, etc.

Mix the Drinks

Put the following lists on the board or a chart and have the children pick one ingredient from each group to use in a recipe. This might be good to do the first time the children try designing a drink.

A	B
7-Up	Lemonade
Club soda	Limeade
Gingerale	Cranberry juice
Sprite	Grapefruit juice
Orange soda	Lemon juice
	Lime juice

C

Orange juice
Pineapple juice
Apple juice
Apricot nectar
Grape juice

Frozen Banana Pops

¼ banana for each child

175 ml chocolate chips

45 ml margarine

Peel each banana and cut into quarters. Put a popsicle stick into each segment. Place on a cookie sheet and freeze. Melt chocolate chips and margarine over low heat. Remove from heat. Dip frozen bananas into chocolate mixture. Cover a cookie sheet with waxed paper. Put chocolate-covered bananas on the cookie sheet and return to freezer. After the bananas are refrozen, they are ready to eat.

From *Recipes for Learning* by Gail Lewis and Jean M. Shaw, ©1979 by Goodyear Publishing Company, Inc.

Frozen Banana Pops

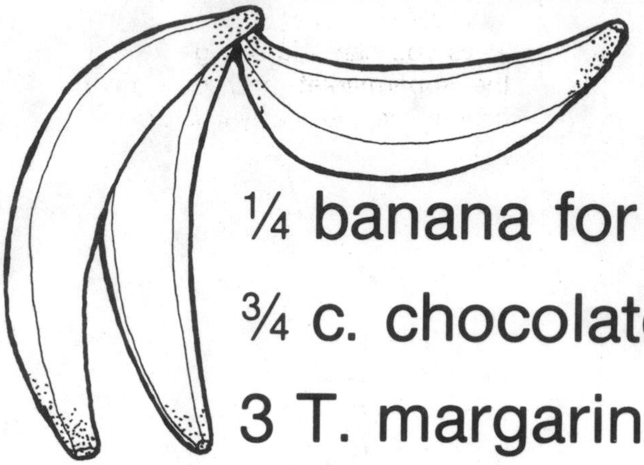

¼ banana for each child

¾ c. chocolate chips

3 T. margarine

Peel each banana and cut into quarters. Put a popsicle stick into each segment. Place on a cookie sheet and freeze. Melt chocolate chips and margarine over low heat. Remove from heat. Dip frozen bananas into chocolate mixture. Cover a cookie sheet with waxed paper. Put chocolate-covered bananas on the cookie sheet and return to freezer. After the bananas are refrozen, they are ready to eat.

From *Recipes for Learning* by Gail Lewis and Jean M. Shaw, ©1979 by Goodyear Publishing Company, Inc.

The following recipes are contained in this section. You may wish to use all of these over a period of time or choose only a few:

Frozen Banana Pops
Fresh Orange Juice
Orange Bowl Salad
Fruit Dip
Sequence Salad
Silly Salads

Refer to individual recipes that you plan to use for equipment and ingredients. This section offers many opportunities for development of five senses, nutritional information, fruits—their history, uses, how they are grown, their size, shape, taste, smell, color, weight, and texture. Plant seeds. Grow an avocado. Put seeds into sets. Use seeds for a seed collage.
Worksheets in Chapter 7 can be used with these recipes.

FRUIT FUN 13

Fresh Orange Juice

Many children have never seen fresh orange juice prepared. Bring a juice squeezer to school and let them take turns squeezing orange juice. Make a list of the different ways you can find orange juice in the supermarket (frozen, bottled, canned, etc.) and why it is good for you.

FRUIT FUN 14

Silly Salads

The children's cards contain four "Silly Salad" recipes. Let the children design other silly salads with real fruit, magazine pictures, or construction paper cutouts. You may wish to send these ideas home. These snacks are fun and nutritious.

FRUIT FUN 15

"Feely" Box

Cut a hole in the side of a medium-sized box, and put several fruits inside the box. Have the children feel the fruits and guess what they are. They can look inside the box to see if they are correct. The fruit can be changed periodically. Try to introduce new and unusual fruits as well as familiar ones.

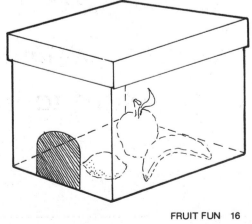

FRUIT FUN 16

35

Orange Bowl Salad

Use halved orange rinds for bowls. Cut up fruit to serve in them. Whipped topping is good on top!

Favorite Fruit Graph

Give each child a 2-inch (5 cm) square of paper. Ask them to draw and color their favorite fruit on their squares. Make a bar graph to determine the group's favorite fruit.

Mix and Match

Obtain a variety of fruits and their seeds. Tape or glue the seeds to 4-inch squares of cardboard. Let the children use these for a game in which the children match seeds to fruit. You can write the answers on the backs of the cards or use pictures on the backs for young children. Young children could also match pictures to real fruit. You should have an assortment of seeds, from very small to large. Does a seed's size determine a fruit's size? (For example, watermelon seed vs. peach seed.) These can be used with "Fruit Compute."

36

Fruit Compute

Make the computer using the directions on the back of this card. Use the mix-and-match cards your teacher made or make other cards for the computer. The cards should be 10 cm square. The question should be on one side and the answer on the back.

FRUIT COMPUTER

Magic Raisins

Drop a few raisins into a fresh glass of gingerale and watch them sink. As gas bubbles form on the raisins, they will rise to the surface. What happens next? Why? (The answer is at the bottom of this card.)

Soon more bubbles gather on the raisins and they rise again. At first, the raisins had no bubbles and were heavier than the volume of soda they displaced. But as the raisins become covered with bubbles, they become lighter than the volume of soda they displace—so they float!

37

From *Recipes for Learning* by Gail Lewis and Jean M. Shaw, ©1979 by Goodyear Publishing Company, Inc.

Computer Directions

(Your teacher may need to help with the cutting.)
Cut two slits in a shoe-box lid using the metric measurements indicated. Cut a 12 cm by 28 cm paper strip and paste it to the top of one slit on the inside of the lid. Tape the lid onto the box and decorate with fruit pictures. Put your question card in the top slot. It will come out the bottom with the answer side up.

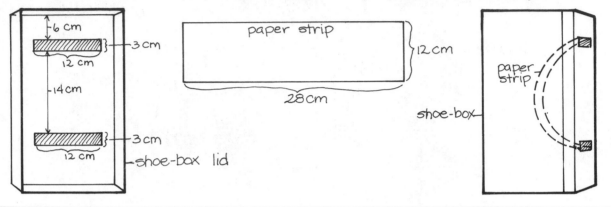

Fruit Dip

You will need:

dry edible ingredients (such as dry cocoa or instant chocolate mix, dry Jell-O, dry Kool-Aid, shredded coconut, dry pudding mix, powdered sugar, brown or white sugar, cinnamon, granola, carob powder), banana and apple slices (or other fruit), small paper cups or bowls, toothpicks.

Take your cups and put a small amount of a dry ingredient into each one. Stick a toothpick in a fruit slice and dip it into one or more of your dry ingredients. Taste them. Which do you like best? Why?

38

From *Recipes for Learning* by Gail Lewis and Jean M. Shaw, ©1979 by Goodyear Publishing Company, Inc.

Silly Salad #1

You will need: cheese, celery, peach, marshmallow, raisins, cherry, lettuce

shredded cheese

marshmallow

lettuce

raisins

celery

peach

celery

Silly Salad #2

You will need: pear halves, raisins, red cinnamon candy or red cherry, carrots or blanched almonds, marshmallow or cottage cheese

eyes:	raisins
ears:	carrots or almonds
mouth:	cinnamon candy or cherry
nose:	raisin
tail:	marshmallow or cottage cheese
body:	pear halves

Silly Salad #3

You will need: lettuce, sliced pineapple, banana, cherry, toothpick

cherry with toothpick —

peeled banana cut in half—

Surprise! A Rocket Salad

lettuce—

pineapple

Silly Salad #4

You will need: pear, prune, orange segment or mandarin orange segments, cherry, raisin

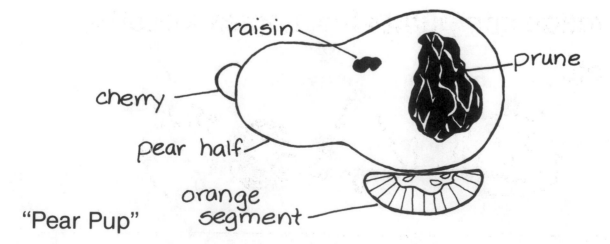

raisin—

—prune

cherry—

pear half—

orange segment—

40   "Pear Pup"

From *Recipes for Learning* by Gail Lewis and Jean M. Shaw, ©1979 by Goodyear Publishing Company, Inc.

Peanut Butter Candy

100 g peanut butter

1 stick margarine

454 g powdered sugar

15 ml vanilla flavoring

food coloring

Blend together peanut butter, margarine, and sugar. Add vanilla. Roll with hands to make shapes like the ones below. Food coloring may be added if desired. This candy can be made into pumpkins, apples, wreaths, etc.

From *Recipes for Learning* by Gail Lewis and Jean M. Shaw, ©1979 by Goodyear Publishing Company, Inc.

Peanut Butter Candy

3 oz. peanut butter

1 stick margarine

1 lb. powdered sugar

1 T. vanilla flavoring

food coloring

Blend together peanut butter, margarine, sugar and vanilla. Roll with hands to make shapes like the ones below. Food coloring may be added if desired. This candy can be made into pumpkins, apples, wreaths, etc.

Equipment List

- Bowl
- Spoon
- Waxed paper or plates for candy

Shopping List

- Peanut butter
- Powdered sugar
- Margarine
- Vanilla
- Food coloring

Information to Share

- The peanut is really a kind of pea, not a nut.
- There are usually two peanuts in every pod (shell).
- Some other names for peanuts are: groundnuts, goobers, goober peas, and pindas.
- George Washington Carver found over 300 uses for the peanut.
  The peanut is used for food, in industry, and on farms.

Number Sentences

Have the children cut out the folding peanuts in Chapter 7 (page 151). Each peanut has a numeral on the outside. The children can put an appropriate number sentence on the inside. These can be stored in envelopes and used for drill, etc. The children can note which combinations have the same answer. Examples:

Learning About Assembly Lines

Use the Peanut Butter Candy recipe to help the children understand assembly lines. The recipe can be quadrupled so that all the children in the class will have small bags or boxes of candy to take home as gifts for their families. The children should know that "assemble" means to put together. The assembly can be made much faster when it is broken down into parts:

1st part: Measure the ingredients.

2nd part: Mix the ingredients.

3rd part: Several children roll candy into 1-inch balls.

4th part: Several children cut 4-inch squares of plastic wrap.

5th part: Several children wrap the candy.

(continued on back)

Word Concentration

Xerox and cut out peanut cards in the cutout section of Chapter 7 (page 151) for a word concentration game. The cards should be placed, words down, in five rows of four cards each. One player starts and turns over two cards. If they match, the player keeps them. Alternate turns for every play even if a player makes a match.

Variations: Younger children can match the words without turning them down.
Other peanut cards can be made by the children to study number words, new vocabulary, colors, etc.

43

Boiled Peanuts

Take raw unshelled peanuts. Boil in water with ¼ cup salt for 1 hour. Turn heat off, cover, and let sit 1 to 2 hours. Shell and eat.

Suggestions

• Taste, touch, and smell ingredients before making candy.

• Talk about how peanut butter can be used.

• Talk about why peanut food products are nutritious foods.

• Watch the consistency and color changes as the ingredients are mixed.

• Use only the primary colors in the food coloring and let the children mix the other colors they want.

• Let the children use the Peanut Butter Candy worksheet in Chapter 7 (page 175) with the recipe.

Things to Do with Peanuts

1. Plant seeds (raw peanuts).
2. Find a growing peanut plant to put on display.
3. Boil raw peanuts.
4. Roast raw peanuts.
5. Read a book about peanuts.

(continued from front)

6th part: Count out a predetermined number of pieces of candy onto each paper square.

What other classroom jobs or other cooking activities could be done in an assembly line?

Things to Study

1. History of the peanut.
2. Use of the peanut.
3. Use of the peanut shell.
4. Nutritional value of the peanut.

From *Recipes for Learning* by Gail Lewis and Jean M. Shaw, ©1979 by Goodyear Publishing Company, Inc.

A Homemade Spinner

Materials needed: 1 golf tee, 1 small margarine "tub," 1 small piece cardboard or a styrofoam meat tray, felt-tip marker, paper punch, ruler, and scissors.

Procedure: Make a cardboard of styrofoam spinner using the pattern on the right. Punch a hole in the large end. Divide the lid of the "tub" into four parts and number each with a felt-tip marker. Attach the spinner to the top of the lid with a golf tee. Use this with your Peanut Patch Game in Chapter 7 (page 174).

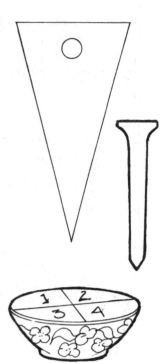

Homemade Peanut Butter
(a picture recipe)

Put [1 CUP] [1 CUP] [1 CUP] of SALT ed into a . Cover and blend for 10 seconds. Add margarine. Blend until smooth.

You may need to stop the blender several times and scrape the sides with a RUBBER SCRAPER .

45

From *Recipes for Learning* by Gail Lewis and Jean M. Shaw, ©1979 by Goodyear Publishing Company, Inc.

A Game Center

Make a game center in your room. Use construction paper, cardboard, crayons, magic markers, etc., to make up your own game to leave in the center. Be sure to put directions on the back of your game so your classmates can also play.

Some ways to use your homemade peanut butter:

celery + peanut butter = celery snacks

apple slices + peanut butter = walking salads

bread + peanut butter + banana slices =

one good sandwich!

46   Add your idea for a peanut butter snack   +   =

From *Recipes for Learning* by Gail Lewis and Jean M. Shaw, ©1979 by Goodyear Publishing Company, Inc.

homemade bubbles

125 ml liquid detergent

500 ml water

30 ml glycerin or salad oil

Mix gently. Use for blowing bubbles.

Suggested "bubblers:"

straws

spools

twisted wire

string with straw handles

squeeze bottle

47

From *Recipes for Learning* by Gail Lewis and Jean M. Shaw, ©1979 by Goodyear Publishing Company, Inc.

homemade bubbles

½ c. liquid detergent

2 c. water

2 T. glycerin or salad oil

Mix gently. Use for blowing bubbles.

Suggested "bubblers:"

straws

spools

twisted wire

string with straw handles

squeeze bottle

From *Recipes for Learning* by Gail Lewis and Jean M. Shaw, ©1979 by Goodyear Publishing Company, Inc.

The following supplies are for all of the soapsud recipes. See the individual recipes for specific amounts.

Equipment List

- Electric mixer or hand beater
- Large bowls
- Spoon
- Measuring spoons and cups
- Construction paper

Shopping List

- Bar soap
- Ivory Snow or similar
- Ivory Snow or similar soap powder (many detergents will *not* work)
- Food coloring (dry tempera paints can be used instead)
- Shaving cream
- Dark washcloths

Soap Sculpture

Fill a large bowl half full of Ivory Snow. Add water gradually while beating with an electric mixer or hand beater until the suds are stiff. Let stand overnight. The mixture will be ready to use for modeling the following day.

Suggestions

- Use to make snowmen, snow creatures.

- Let dry and then carve with plastic knives, popsicle sticks, etc. as you would carve a bar of soap.

- Add food coloring for a colored "clay."

- An individual recipe for a child to prepare alone is on one of the children's cards.

Washcloth Painting

This can be done as a large-group activity if each child brings one dark-colored washcloth. If done as a small-group activity, you may wish to purchase several dark washcloths. Each cloth should be thoroughly wet. The children run a bar of soap back and forth on a washcloth, which is spread out on a desk or table. With their hands, they rub the cloth until it is sudsy. Then they can draw pictures in the suds with their fingers. The drawings can be erased by resudsing and the cloth used again.

Soap Paint
(two parts soap, one part water)

Mix Ivory Snow and water and beat until it is the consistency of whipped cream. Divide the mixture up into paper cups, small bowls, or glasses. Add food coloring to each container for desired color. The children can use this mixture as they would any paint with brushes.

49

Suggestions

- Let the children compare textures of soap before and after mixture is made.

- Use to study color changes—for example, yellow + red = orange.

- Compare the use of an electric beater with a hand beater.

- Study units of measurement.

- Add oil of peppermint, oil of cloves, etc. for an added sensory experience.

Suggestions

- Food coloring makes the paint pastels; tempera will give you darker colors.

- You can use this paint to paint letters and numerals on cardboard. After they dry they can be used for "touch" cards.

Suggestions

- Use this idea for practice on manuscript, cursive, or formation of numerals.

- Use for math drill or spelling practice.

- Good for any prewriting activity.

From *Recipes for Learning* by Gail Lewis and Jean M. Shaw, ©1979 by Goodyear Publishing Company, Inc.

Soap Sculpture

¾ c. (175 ml) Ivory Snow
1 T. (15 ml) water

Mix with an electric beater until stiff. Make anything you would like. Let dry.

This makes enough for one person. Can you write down a recipe to be used with two people? Three?

Make a Cake!

Mix up Ivory Snow with water and beat with an electric beater until the consistency of icing. Use this as it is or color it with food coloring to frost a "cake." Your cake can be a shoe box, oatmeal box, etc. Cut it the size you want and turn it upside down. Ice and decorate with: sticks, macaroni, plastic flowers, leaves, beads, buttons, etc.

DO NOT EAT!!

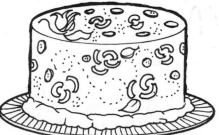

51

From *Recipes for Learning* by Gail Lewis and Jean M. Shaw, ©1979 by Goodyear Publishing Company, Inc.

Shaving Cream Fingerpaint

You will need: 1 can shaving cream or several partially full cans.

Squirt shaving cream on any slick surface: desk, table, paper, cookie sheet, oil cloth, etc. Spread out on smooth surface with hands. Paint with fingers and/or hands. If your teacher says "OK," you might try adding tempera (dry) or food colors.

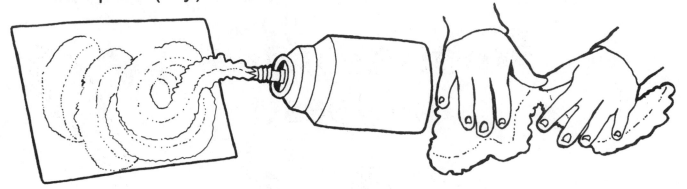

Snow

Mix one part water with two parts Ivory Snow. Beat until it looks like whipped cream. Use for snow pictures. Use this mixture on your Christmas tree for pretend snow. Take a handful and rub on the branches. Let dry.

52

From *Recipes for Learning* by Gail Lewis and Jean M. Shaw, ©1979 by Goodyear Publishing Company, Inc.

CHAPTER
FOUR

Small-Appliance Recipes

Applesauce

½ apple for each person

½ stick cinnamon

125 ml water

125 ml sugar

3 ml nutmeg

Core, peel, and quarter apples. Boil in water with cinnamon 15-25 minutes. Add sugar and nutmeg. Mix well. Mash, using hand mixer or wire whisk or potato masher. Serve in small paper cups.

From *Recipes for Learning* by Gail Lewis and Jean M. Shaw, ©1979 by Goodyear Publishing Company, Inc.

Applesauce

½ apple for each person

½ stick cinnamon

½ c. water

½ c. sugar

½ t. nutmeg

Core, peel, and quarter apples. Boil in water with cinnamon 15-25 minutes. Add sugar and nutmeg. Mix well. Mash, using hand mixer or wire whisk or potato masher. Serve in small paper cups.

Equipment List

- Large saucepan
- Wooden spoons
- Hot plate
- Beater, wire whisk, or potato masher
- Apple corer
- Potato peeler
- Paring knife

Shopping List

- Apples
- Sugar
- Nutmeg
- Cinnamon
- Small paper cups and plastic spoons

Notes

This recipe is one that lends itself to using with a large group since each child can take part in preparing the apples. *(continued on back)*

APPLESAUCE 25

Mr. Applehead
(oral communication)

Cut two large apples from construction paper. Cut features like those on back. Make sure that you make two sets of each feature. Two children sit facing each other with a book or screen between them. Each child should have an apple and a complete set of features. One child is the sender and the other is the receiver. The sender tells the receiver what features to put where. After he or she is through, the children check to see if the appleheads look the same.

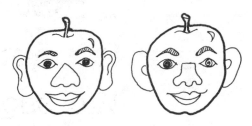

APPLESAUCE 26

A Sharing Salad

Have each person in the class bring one fruit. Peel, clean, dice and toss to make a sharing salad. Add  to keep it from turning brown before it is eaten.

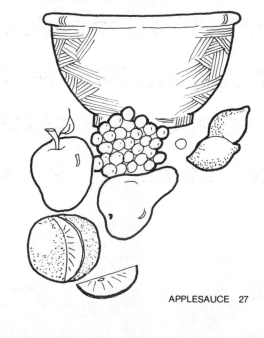

APPLESAUCE 27

Fruit Printing

Materials:  s, s, s. , paper towels, plain paper and paint.

Procedure: Cut each piece of fruit in half. Pour paint into a paper plate, pie tin, or large lid. Make sure that the paint is spread evenly over the plate, tin, or lid. Dip the cut side of the fruit in the paint. Lift and press the painted fruit onto the plain paper. Lift carefully and look at the print. Make a design with different prints.

Try printing on other surfaces: newspaper, old wallpaper, etc.

APPLESAUCE 28

57

From *Recipes for Learning* by Gail Lewis and Jean M. Shaw, ©1979 by Goodyear Publishing Company, Inc.

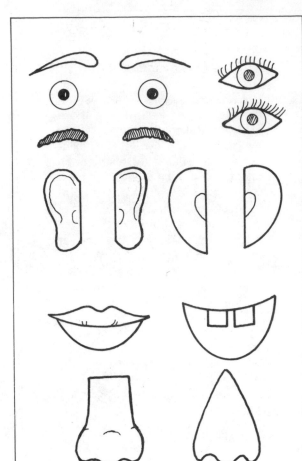

(continued from front)

Let the children decide how many apples they will need if the recipe calls for half an apple per person. The apples can be quartered and then each child can peel and remove the core and seeds for his or her two parts.

Suggestions

- Bring in different kinds of apples and compare their look, taste, size.
- Compare apple seeds to other seeds and classify the different kinds of seeds.
- Have a lesson on "half" and let children divide other things into halves.
- Let the children find pictures of recipes using apples in them.
- Find pictures of apples and other fruit.
- Bring recipes from home containing apples. Make an apple cookbook for a gift (Mother's Day, Christmas).

Apple Puzzles

Make apples out of construction paper. Cut each apple in half so that it can be put together only with its matching piece. Use these for letter match, numeral-number match, compound words, etc.

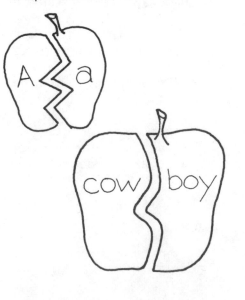

"Apple of My Eye" Bulletin Board (self-concept)

Let each child make a large apple with his or her name on it. All the children add what they think is special about each person and tack it under the appropriate apple.

58

Apple Relay

Divide the children into two teams and give each team one apple. Each team leader holds the apple under his or her chin and must pass the apple to the next child's neck, using no hands. The apple is passed to each child this way. The first team to finish is the winner.

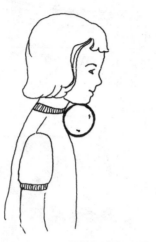

APPLE ACTIVITIES 29

Fruity People

Let the children cut out all kinds of fruits from magazines and put them in a box. The children then glue these pictures on paper to make "Fruity People." Features can be added with crayons.

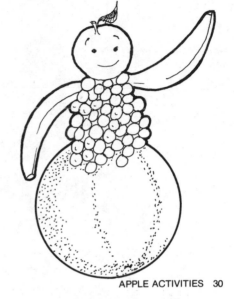

APPLE ACTIVITIES 30

Cinnamon-Centimeter

Divide the children into two teams. Give each child a paper ruler with centimeters marked on it. Give each team one stick of cinnamon. Each child measures the stick cinnamon, and the team decides on the correct measurement. The first team to report the correct measurement to the teacher wins.

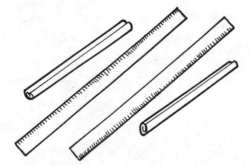

APPLE ACTIVITIES 31

Guess the Spice

Let a small group of children smell and taste various spices as they learn each spice's name. After the children feel they know each spice, blindfold one child at a time and let him or her guess, by smelling, what each spice is.
Suggested spices: nutmeg, cinnamon, cloves, ginger, pumpkin pie spice.

Match by Smell

Have the following for the children to match:
Stick cinnamon to ground cinnamon — Whole cloves to ground cloves — Whole allspice to allspice — Peppercorns to pepper

APPLE ACTIVITIES 32

A Measuring Activity

Use pictures of fruit cut out of magazines for metric measuring. The children can use a metric ruler to find out the width and length of the pictures.

Write Your Own Recipe

Give each child a "write your own recipe" sheet with instructions to find a recipe using apples—either at home or at school. These recipes can be illustrated and put together in an Apple Cookbook. The children may want to make copies to use as gifts.

A Cinnamon-Stick Ruler

Let the children measure objects in the room by cinnamon sticks. Examples: A book is____cinnamon sticks long.
My chair is____cinnamon sticks tall. This activity helps children understand that metric or standard measurement depends on a unit or standard.

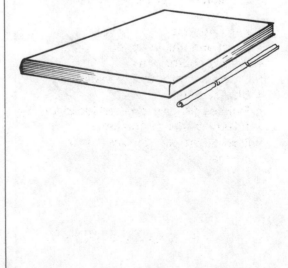

From *Recipes for Learning* by Gail Lewis and Jean M. Shaw, ©1979 by Goodyear Publishing Company, Inc.

Poetry Center

The children might like to paint a large tree and copy poems about apples on red construction-paper apples. Some children may want to find other poems or write their own to hang on the tree.

APPLE POETRY CENTER   33

Apple Poems

Make a class book of apple poems. Start with the ones in this section, and then collect others from books and magazines. Encourage the children to write more apple poems. Copy the poems neatly and compile them in a class book.

A was once an apple pie,
Pidy,
Widy,
Tidy,
Pidy,
Nice insidy,
Apple pie!

B was once a little bear,
Beary,
Wary,
Hairy,
Beary
Take cary,
Little bear!   *(continued on back)*

APPLE POETRY CENTER   34

Suggestions for Children at Poetry Center

1. Read a poem to a friend.
2. Write a poem of your own.
3. Illustrate a poem.
4. Copy a poem in your best handwriting.

Materials for Poetry Center

- Poetry books
- Lined and unlined paper
- Pencils and/or pens
- Crayons and/or magic markets
- Display area
- Pictures (to give children ideas for subject matter of poems)
- Illustrations of various kinds of poems

APPLE POETRY CENTER   35

Apple Match Up

Practice compound words or math facts on "apple" parts. Cut out apple shapes or let the children do it. Write halves of compound words on different parts of the apple, or write problems and answers. Cut in half. Shuffle parts. Have the children match them.

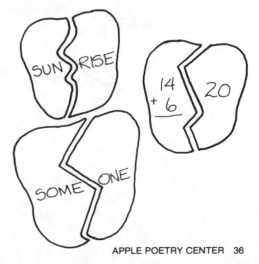

APPLE POETRY CENTER   36

From *Recipes for Learning* by Gail Lewis and Jean M. Shaw, ©1979 by Goodyear Publishing Company, Inc.

(continued from front)

C was once a little
Caky,
Baky,
Maky
Caky
Taky caky, little cake!

Poem by Edward Lear

The Apple Tree (finger play)

Way up high in the apple tree,
(hands way up)

Two little apples smiled at me.
(point to smile)

I shook the tree as hard as I could,
(shake hands)

Down came the apples.
(hands flutter down)

Ummm, they were good.
(rub stomach)

Apple

A . . . Appetizing crispness.
P . . . Pomme in French.
P . . . Peel it or not.
L . . . Love it fresh and cold.
E . . . Eve's temptation.
Apple.

An Experiment— Oxidation

Take an apple and cut it in half. Pour lemon juice over one half. Leave both halves in the air. Watch for changes. Write down what happens.

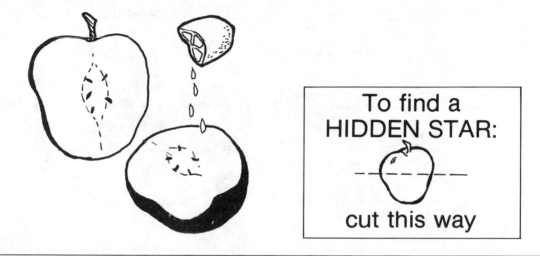

To find a
HIDDEN STAR:

cut this way

Walking Salad

Take an apple half, one spoonful of peanut butter, raisins, and miniature marshmallows and create your own salad.

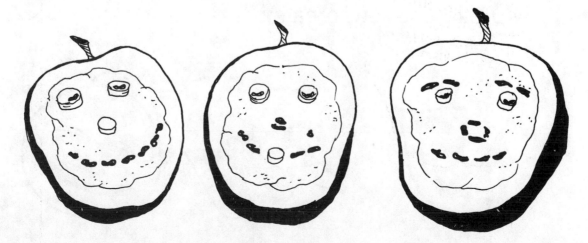

63

From *Recipes for Learning* by Gail Lewis and Jean M. Shaw, ©1979 by Goodyear Publishing Company, Inc.

A Hidden Star

If you cut an apple exactly right,
You'll find a star hidden from sight.
Now make a wish with your eyes closed tight.
(If you need help, look on the other side of this card.)

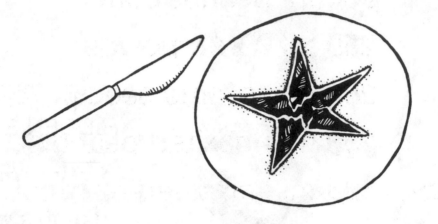

Fruit People

Materials needed: apples, oranges, lemons, raisins, raw vegetables, toothpicks, etc.
Procedure: Use toothpicks to attach features to the fruit. You can eat your creation.

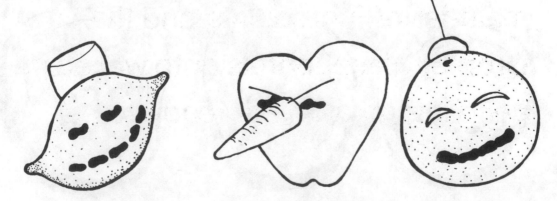

64

Carob Candy

250 ml honey

250 ml peanut butter

250 ml carob powder

250 ml sesame seeds

250 ml unsalted peanuts

125 ml shredded coconut

125 ml chopped dried fruit

Heat honey and peanut butter until they can be easily mixed together. Quickly add carob powder and the remainder of ingredients and then mix. Drop by teaspoonfuls onto waxed paper. Refrigerate until ready to eat.

From *Recipes for Learning* by Gail Lewis and Jean M. Shaw, ©1979 by Goodyear Publishing Company, Inc.

Carob Candy

1 c. honey

1 c. peanut butter

1 c. carob powder

1 c. sesame seeds

1 c. unsalted peanuts

½ c. shredded coconut

½ c. chopped dried fruit

Heat honey and peanut butter until they can be easily mixed together. Quickly add carob powder and the remainder of the ingredients and then mix. Drop by teaspoonfuls onto waxed paper. Refrigerate until ready to eat.

From *Recipes for Learning* by Gail Lewis and Jean M. Shaw, ©1979 by Goodyear Publishing Company, Inc.

Equipment List

- Hot plate
- Large saucepan
- Large spoon
- Waxed paper

Shopping List

- Honey
- Peanut butter
- Carob powder ⎫ (try a health food
- Sesame seeds ⎭ store for these)
- Unsalted peanuts
- Shredded coconut
- Dried fruit
  (dates, raisins, etc.)

Information

Carob looks and tastes very much like cocoa. Children can eat it even if they are allergic to chocolate.

CAROB CANDY

CAROB CANDY 37

Sensory Words

Let the children dictate words to describe each ingredient in the Carob Candy recipe. Put the ingredients out on a table and have the children see if they can find where the words would go. Will the words apply to more than one ingredient?

Experience Chart

With the class, make an experience chart about seeds we eat. Try to get as many responses as possible. (The Children may not realize that some foods such as rice, corn, and peas are seeds.) Leave space for an example of each seed to be glued or taped next to the word.

CAROB CANDY 38

How Much Is a Cup?

Let the children use metric or standard scales to weigh the ingredients by the cup. Be sure you use the same kind of cup each time. Use the worksheet in Chapter 7 (page 178) and let the children fill out their worksheets as they weigh.

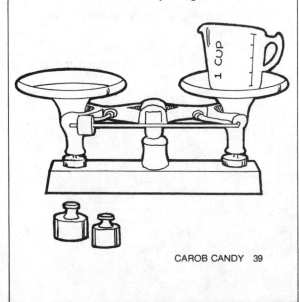

CAROB CANDY 39

Research Project

Find out the likenesses and differences of these trees:

> Cacao tree
> Carob tree
> Coconut palm

The children may want to write up their findings or draw a picture of each tree.

CAROB CANDY 40

67

From *Recipes for Learning* by Gail Lewis and Jean M. Shaw, ©1979 by Goodyear Publishing Company, Inc.

Suggestions

- Compare taste and appearance of carob and cocoa. Talk about each ingredient, its origin, taste, uses, and what could be substituted (example: sugar or molasses for honey, cocoa for carob).

- What ingredients determine the color, taste, and consistency of the candy?

- Look at the honeycomb in some jars of honey.

- Make your own peanut butter.

- Bring a coconut to share.

Research Project

Find other uses for:
    Peanuts
    Coconuts and coconut palms
    Carob

Word and Letter Games

(Using words on page 152 in Chapter 7.)
1. Provide duplicate words for the ingredients and have the children match them to the recipe.
2. Put the words into alphabetical order.
3. Find all the words that begin with blends.
4. Divide the words into syllables.
5. Find smaller words hidden in the larger words.

From *Recipes for Learning* by Gail Lewis and Jean M. Shaw, ©1979 by Goodyear Publishing Company, Inc.

Peanut Shell Finger Puppets

Find some peanut shells to use as finger puppets. Carefully break off one end of the shell so that it can be slipped onto your fingertip. You may add features with magic markers, paint, or colored pencils. Yarn, string, and fabric scraps are good to use for hair, clothes, and other features.

(continued on back)

Shopping List

Make a picture shopping list by cutting out food pictures from magazines or newspapers. Find out the prices of your food products next time you go grocery shopping or look in the grocery ad section of your newspaper.

69

(continued from front)

A puppet stage can be made by folding a sheet of heavy paper into thirds and cutting a hole for the stage opening. You may wish to write a story to present with your finger puppets. Your story could be about good nutrition and answer these questions:

1. Why is refined sugar not always the best sweetener for you?
2. Why are peanuts nutritious snacks?

Peanut People

Make your own peanut people out of brown construction paper. Draw in "people" features or cut them out of magazines. You may want to add other things such as:

• Fruit for ears, eyes, nose, hair, etc.
• Nuts for feet, hands, etc.

From *Recipes for Learning* by Gail Lewis and Jean M. Shaw, ©1979 by Goodyear Publishing Company, Inc.

Charades

Find a friend to play with. Choose one ingredient from the Carob Candy recipe and see if you can act out enough clues so your friend can guess what it is.

"C" and "Y"

Write a creative story about "C" and "Y."

_____
_____
_____
_____
_____
_____
_____
_____

From _Recipes for Learning_ by Gail Lewis and Jean M. Shaw, ©1979 by Goodyear Publishing Company, Inc.

Candy Sale

Have a candy sale at your school. Put the money you make in your cooking fund for the expenses of your class's cooking activity.

People you might sell to: parents (at a parents' meeting), classmates (after lunch), teachers.

Make a Candy Graph

You and your classmates each bring a wrapper from your favorite candy. Make a bar graph to see which are the most popular candy bars in your class. If someone forgets to bring a wrapper, make one out of paper.

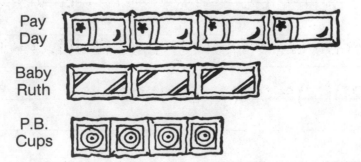

From *Recipes for Learning* by Gail Lewis and Jean M. Shaw, ©1979 by Goodyear Publishing Company, Inc.

finger Jell-o

4 pkgs. unflavored gelatin

500 ml hot water

2 small pkgs. flavored gelatin

500 ml cold water

What to do:

Stir unflavored gelatin into 100 ml hot water. Let soften about 15 minutes. Add flavored gelatin and 400 ml hot water. Stir until well dissolved. Add cold water. Very lightly grease a 22 x 30 cm pan or spray with a vegetable shortening. Pour gelatin in. Refrigerate until gelatin is firm.

From *Recipes for Learning* by Gail Lewis and Jean M. Shaw, ©1979 by Goodyear Publishing Company, Inc.

finger jell-o

4 pkgs. unflavored gelatin

2 c. hot water

2 small pkgs. flavored gelatin

2 c. cold water

What to do:

Stir unflavored gelatin into ½ c. hot water. Let soften about 15 minutes. Add flavored gelatin and 1½ c. hot water. Stir until well dissolved. Add cold water. Very lightly grease a 9 x 13 in. pan or spray with a vegetable shortening. Pour gelatin in. Refrigerate until gelatin is firm.

74

From *Recipes for Learning* by Gail Lewis and Jean M. Shaw, ©1979 by Goodyear Publishing Company, Inc.

Equipment List

- Two mixing bowls or large measuring cups
- Measuring cups
- Medium saucepan
- Mixing spoons
- Hot plate or stove
- Hot pads
- 9 × 13 pan

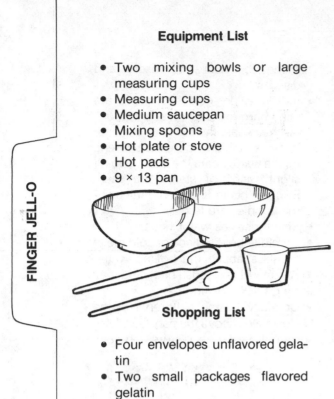

Shopping List

- Four envelopes unflavored gelatin
- Two small packages flavored gelatin
- Salad oil or vegetable spray

FINGER JELLO 41

Variations for Finger Jell-O

Let the children try these variations.
- Mix different colors of gelatin and see what happens.
- Add bits of chopped fruit, grated carrot, chopped nuts or coconut.
- Mash firm gelatin with a fork and serve the "shreds" in a bowl or paper cup.
- While it is still warm, whip gelatin with an egg beater.
- Your idea:_____

Ways to Cut Finger Jell-O

(Be sure to save and eat the scraps too!)
- Rectangles
- Squares
- Circles or donuts
- Letters or numerals
- Diamonds
- "Snakes"
- Cookie cutters

FINGER JELLO 42

Sensory Experiences
Gelatin and Other Substances

Feel Them
Put small amounts of grainy substances in containers. Gelatin, salt cornmeal, sand, and celery seed could be used. Let the children feel the various substances, describe what they feel, and discuss similarities and differences. Boxes that discourage peeking are fun—use coffee cans, cereal boxes, or sock-covered half-pint containers.

Taste Them
Let volunteers taste gelatin, flavored gelatin, sugar, salt, cornmeal, and celery seed and try to tell which is which. Blindfolding the taster or having him close his eyes adds to the suspense.

FINGER JELLO 43

Jell-O Poll

Let pupils poll their classmates to find out favorite gelatin colors or flavors, with one or two children in charge. They ask each of their classmates about preferred gelatin flavors or colors, and record the results. Then they make a graph of the results. The children can draw a bar graph (as shown), picturegraph, or paste on squares of colored paper. Display and discuss the results.

Jell-O Box Geometry

Count the flat surfaces of a gelatin box. Carefully open the box and count again. Trace the shape onto construction paper. Cut out and carefully fold the shape to make your own box. Tape or glue the edges. Name the shapes.

FINGER JELLO 44

75

From *Recipes for Learning* by Gail Lewis and Jean M. Shaw, ©1979 by Goodyear Publishing Company, Inc.

Information

- Gelatin is a protein substance made from bones and the skins of animals. It is hard, colorless, and tasteless. To make gelatin, bones and skins are heated and treated with chemicals. The gelatin is concentrated, chilled, sliced, and ground.

- Gelatin is easily digested by sick persons or babies, so it makes a good food for a "light" diet. Gelatin is protein, but when mixed with sugar, flavoring, and water, its main food value is a carbohydrate.

- Gelatin is used to coat medicines and photo papers, and as a medium for growing bacteria.

Observations

Things for children to observe and discuss:
- Individual dry gelatin particles are fairly hard and have a slight odor.
- As they soak, the particles become larger, softer, and more transparent.
- As the water nears the boiling point, slight wisps of steam are seen.
- Bubbles begin to rise. At "full boil," the bubbles are larger.
- Steam rises as water boils.
- Carefully hold a piece of cold metal or glass above the boiling water.
- Steam will condense on it, and may "rain back" into the pan.
- Carefully let the children feel the steam well above the pan. Careful—it's hot! Feel the moisture and heat.

Language Experience

After the children have had the experience of working with and eating finger gelatin, lead a discussion or make lists of things involving some properties of the gelatin and its ingredients. For example:
- Grainy things
- Things that dissolve
- Things we can cut easily
- "Rubbery" things
- Sweet things
- Things we eat with our fingers

Smell and Tell

- Blindfold the children or have them close their eyes.

- Have them take turns smelling flavored and unflavored gelatins to see if they can tell the difference.

- Let the children smell fruit-flavored gelatin and real fruit. They can then try to match gelatin and fruit by their odor.

- Let the children smell fruit extracts and gelatin of matching flavors and then tell what they smell.

From *Recipes for Learning* by Gail Lewis and Jean M. Shaw, ©1979 by Goodyear Publishing Company, Inc.

Hello Jell-O

Imagine that you have just met a Jell-O creature. What do you say to him after you say "Hello Jell-O?"

Write a story about it! What special problems might a Jell-O creature have? What might he look like? What adventures could you imagine for your Jell-O creature? Draw a picture to go with your story.

Measure . . . Measure . . . Measure

Guess and check the following things from the Finger Jell-O recipes:

	"Guess"	"Check"
1. Length of gelatin box		
2. Width of gelatin envelope		
3. Length of pan		
4. Weight of gelatin envelope		
5. Weight of finger Jell-O and pan		
6. Volume of 1 envelope of gelatin		
7. Volume of flavored gelatin		
8. Volume of pan filled to top		

Create a Jell-O Mobile

Jell-O Mobile #1
Cut pictures of Jell-O from magazines or draw them. Paste onto colored paper. Hang pictures from string or yarn. Suspend strings from sticks, hangers, paper plates.

Jell-O Mobile #2
When is a Jell-O mobile also a car? When you add wheels, headlights, and a driver to a gelatin box! Use construction paper, glue, markers or crayons to make a Jell-O mobile. Wheels may be attached with glue or paper fasteners.

Science Fun with Gelatin

- Set gelatin different ways:
  Use a small amount of mixed-up flavored gelatin. Set some out at room temperature. Set some in the refrigerator and some in the freezer. Record the time you put the Jell-O in the three places. Compare the times on a chart or graph. Will the gelatin set at room temperature?

  Jell-O Setting Times

  Freezer _____

  Refrigerator _____

  Room Temperature _____

- Classify gelatin ads:
  Cut out several gelatin ads. Classify them different ways—by color, fruited or plain, whipped or not, desert or salad, and others.

78

From *Recipes for Learning* by Gail Lewis and Jean M. Shaw, ©1979 by Goodyear Publishing Company, Inc.

Jell-O Box Critters

Gather up some boxes, glue, paper, markers.
Make boxes into people, animals, or creatures.
What other box critters can you make?

Jell-O Box Science: Dissolving Fun

1. List some things that you think will dissolve in water and some that won't dissolve.
2. Check your predictions by stirring small amounts of ingredients in hot and cold water.
3. Try things like salt, flour, sugar, gelatin, wood chips, sand, cornstarch.
4. Tell if things seem to dissolve best in hot or cold water.
5. Ask your teacher if you can dissolve ingredients in a glass pan on the overhead projector. Stir slowly and carefully. Take turns stirring and watching.

79

From *Recipes for Learning* by Gail Lewis and Jean M. Shaw, ©1979 by Goodyear Publishing Company, Inc.

Creative Movement

Try these exercises with your friends:

Jell-O Mix-Up
Pretend to be gelatin in various stages—small, hard gelatin grains, boiling water, gelatin being mixed, cooling gelatin, "stiff" gelatin, gelatin being cut apart.

Shakey Shapes
Remember how gelatin moves? Gently shaking and vibrating. Shakes these body parts just like gelatin—heads, "jelly belly," legs, right arms, both arms. Listen to several "shakey songs" and decide which is best. Now do a shakey walk or shakey run.

Freeze 'n' Melt
Pretend to be regular gelatin, then stiff old gelatin, gelatin that got into the freezer by mistake, then gelatin that got hot and melted.

Jell-O Word Hunt

Challenge a friend in the Jell-O word hunt. Make all the words you can from the letters in Finger Jell-O recipe. Use each letter only once, or the number of times it occurs in the words above. List all the words you can in five minutes, then compare. Some starters:

Finger Jell-o Recipe
in
rip
fill
ring

From *Recipes for Learning* by Gail Lewis and Jean M. Shaw, ©1979 by Goodyear Publishing Company, Inc.

COOKED FINGER PAINT

Stir together in pan:

    250 ml flour

    60 ml salt

Add gradually:

    1250 ml water

Cook over medium heat until thick. Add small amount powdered tempera paint. Use when cool. FUN!

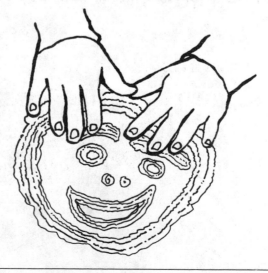

From *Recipes for Learning* by Gail Lewis and Jean M. Shaw, ©1979 by Goodyear Publishing Company, Inc.

COOKED FINGER PAINT

Stir together in pan:

   1 c. flour

   ¼ c. salt

Add gradually:

   5 c. water

Cook over medium heat until thick. Add small amount powdered tempera paint. Use when cool. FUN!

From *Recipes for Learning* by Gail Lewis and Jean M. Shaw, ©1979 by Goodyear Publishing Company, Inc.

Shopping List

- Flour
- Salt
- Powdered tempera

Equipment List

- Pan
- Stove or hot plate
- Measuring cups
- Mixing spoons
- Storage containers

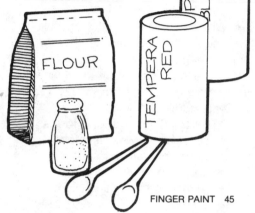

FINGER PAINT 45

Using Finger Paint

- Finger paint is fun but messy. It must be well supervised to be successful.
- Have the children wear smocks, old shirts, or aprons and roll up their sleeves.
- Encourage keeping paint on the paper and table. Praise those who cooperate.
- Have the children work in low, flat pans such as jelly-roll pans or trays. This keeps paint under control.

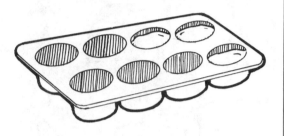

FINGER PAINT 46

Math with Finger Paint

- Dip out paint with a measuring device such as a 15-ml spoon. See how long you can paint with 15 ml of paint.
- See how long a line can be made with 15 ml of paint—really try to stretch it out!
- Weigh the paint when it is done. Use grams or kilograms.
- Add paint 1 gram (a very small amount) at a time.

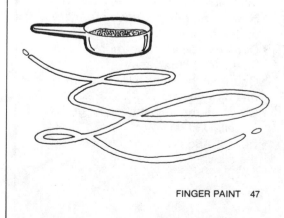

FINGER PAINT 47

Finger Painting Activities

Mixing Colors

- Use two colors of tempera paint when cooking finger paint. Predict the result. Mix and see how it turns out.

- Put two blobs of paint on each child's paper. Have them name the colors and predict what the mixed-up result will be. Mix paint thoroughly with hands.

Group Painting

- Use finger paint on butcher paper on the floor. Let four to six students paint at one time. Compare "strokes" —the way paint is applied.

- Paint to music, using a tape-recorded song or a record.

FINGER PAINT 48

83

Storing Finger Paint

- Store paint in airtight containers. Mayonnaise or peanut butter jars let the color show.
- Children can easily dip paint out of flat containers such as plastic margarine or whipped-cream tubs.
- Paint keeps for at least two or three weeks. Refrigerate for longer storage.
- Dip out paint with plastic spoons or tongue depressors.

Using the Color Clown to Extend Color Concepts

Xerox and cut out the clown in Chapter 7 (page 153). Attach him to a cereal box or milk carton with paper clips. Cut out the balls. Use the clown in many ways:

- Let the clown hold a colored ball. Let children name color or attach another ball with color name.
- Let the clown hold two colored balls and attach the ball that shows the color of mixing the two colors on his foot.
- Write on the plain colored balls and let the children match:
  - math facts and answers (write the operation on the clown's nose)
  - pictures and words
  - contractions and long forms
  - upper and lower case letters
  - coins and values
  - words and definitions
  - animal groups and specific animals

More Finger Painting Activities

- Make a booklet of handprint, footprints, or fingerprints for each child.
- Use different colors for each page.
- Use finger-painted paper as wrapping paper for a special gift.
- Practice handwriting strokes or letters with finger paint—use large, free motions.
- Use combs, sponges, toothbrushes, cardboard, papertowels, or other "findings" to add additional texture to finger painting.
- Make finger paint texture rubs. Put a figure, shape, or letter cut out of cardboard under paper. Finger paint over it. The shapes will show.

Math Tasks for the Color Clown

After you or the children have colored the clown, do tasks such as:

- Count all the red and orange dots on front.
- Count the small blue dots.
- Count the ruffles.
- Count the large red dots.
- Find the difference between the largest and smallest numbers on the clown's trousers.
- How many more blue dots are there than pink dots?
- How many green stripes are there on the front and back?
- Does the clown have more red or blue parts? How many?
- Count all the small dots that aren't green or yellow.
- Count all the dots that aren't green or yellow.
- Bonus! Add up all the numbers on the clown.

From *Recipes for Learning* by Gail Lewis and Jean M. Shaw, ©1979 by Goodyear Publishing Company, Inc.

PANCAKES

(Makes 15-18)

1. 250 ml milk
2. 30 ml melted margarine
3. 1 egg
4. 250 ml sifted flour
5. 10 ml baking powder
6. 30 ml sugar
7. 3 ml salt

Pour 1, 2, and 3 into a large bowl. Beat lightly. Add 4, 5, 6, and 7. Stir all ingredients together. Lightly grease a frying pan or skillet and heat it over medium heat. Pour batter into pan to make the size pancake you want. Turn when bubbles form on top.

From *Recipes for Learning* by Gail Lewis and Jean M. Shaw, ©1979 by Goodyear Publishing Company, Inc.

PANCAKES

(Makes 15-18)

1. 1 c. milk
2. 2 T. melted margarine
3. 1 egg
4. 1 c. sifted flour
5. 2 t. baking powder
6. 2 T. sugar
7. ½ t. salt

Pour 1, 2, and 3 into a large bowl. Beat lightly. Add 4, 5, 6, and 7. Stir all ingredients together. Lightly grease a frying pan or skillet and heat it over medium heat. Pour batter into pan to make the size pancake you want. Turn when bubbles form on top.

From *Recipes for Learning* by Gail Lewis and Jean M. Shaw, ©1979 by Goodyear Publishing Company, Inc.

PANCAKES

Shopping List

(Get enough for two batches)
- Milk
- Margarine
- Flour
- Baking powder
- Sugar
- Salt
- Eggs

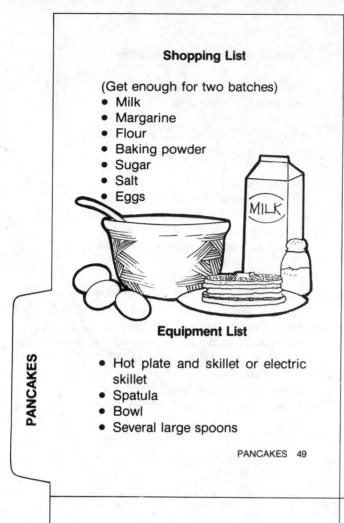

Equipment List

- Hot plate and skillet or electric skillet
- Spatula
- Bowl
- Several large spoons

Flannel Board Math

Cut brown 1½-inch circles from felt. Pose problems in addition, subtraction, multiplication, and division for the children to solve with these felt "pancakes."

Examples:
- Mother cooked three pancakes for herself and four for you. How many did she cook in all?
- We cooked seven pancakes and burned two. How many did we have to eat?
- There are three stacks of pancakes. Each stack has four pancakes in it. How many are there in all?
- There are three pancakes left. Jon and Alice want to eat them. How can they divide them equally?

Pancake People

Cut different sizes of circles from brown construction paper. Arrange them on a piece of paper to make people or animals and paste them down. Use magic markers or crayons to add features or other details. You may want to let the children:
- Name their creation.
- Write a story to go along with it.

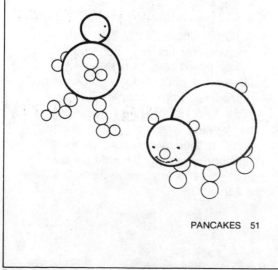

Rhyming Word Race

This can be played with two people or two teams. One person or team uses the word *pan* and the other person or team uses the word *cake*. Both sides start at the same time and write down as many words as they can think of that rhyme with their word. After a certain length of time, the team with the largest number of correct words wins. Set a time limit according to the ages and skills of the children.

From *Recipes for Learning* by Gail Lewis and Jean M. Shaw, ©1979 by Goodyear Publishing Company, Inc.

Fractions

To be used as a teacher-directed activity with the fraction worksheet in Chapter 7 (page 157). For each pancake have the child:

Name the unit (1 pancake)
How many parts to the unit? (2)
Are the parts the same size? (yes)
Tell the child that the one part has a name. It is called_____ (½)

Let the children use the concrete models to explore the relationships between them.

Hints and Information to Share

The way to tell if the pan is hot enough: drop of water will bounce. If the drop sits and boils: not hot enough. If the drop vanishes: too hot.

Questions to ask:
- Which ingredients are dry? Which are liquid?
- As each ingredient is added, talk about its characteristics and how children have used it at home—for example, sugar on cereal.
- How does each ingredient affect the color and consistency of the batter?
- What substitutions could be made? (For example, honey for sugar.)
- When do you eat pancakes? What other foods are similar? How long does it take pancakes to cook?
- Does the size affect the cooking time?

Directions for Pancake Match

Make "pancake match" games for skill development in different areas. The children can match appropriate pairs. Examples:

Visual discrimination
Upper case to lower case
letters — A a
Number to numeral . 1 .. 2 ... 3
Contractions, compound words, math problems and answers, colors to color words, and rhyming words are other suggestions.

Directions for Mystery Ingredients Game

You will need five small clear jars such as baby-food jars. Number the jars 1 through 5. Put a small amount of the following dry ingredients in the jars:

- Flour
- Baking powder
- Sugar
- Salt
- (Other ingredients with similar characteristics may be used. Powdered sugar works well.)

Give each child who is playing a worksheet from Chapter 7 (page 185). They record their guess first by looking, then by looking and shaking, then by smelling, touching, and finally tasting. Provide an answer sheet listing the ingredient in each jar.

From *Recipes for Learning* by Gail Lewis and Jean M. Shaw, ©1979 by Goodyear Publishing Company, Inc.

Pancake Creatures

Prepare pancakes as directed. Dribble batter from a spoon to make any creature or shape you like. Turn with a spatula when pancakes have bubbles on the top. Cook on opposite side. Serve and eat.

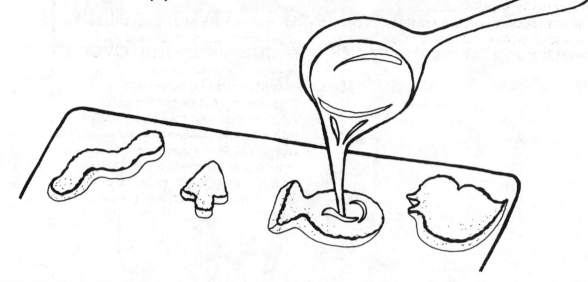

Round as a Pancake . . .

Take an old magazine, scissors, and glue and see how many "round" pictures you can find. Cut and paste these on a sheet of paper. List other things that have a round (circle) shape.

89

From *Recipes for Learning* by Gail Lewis and Jean M. Shaw, ©1979 by Goodyear Publishing Company, Inc.

Pancake Letters

Prepare pancake batter as directed. Dribble batter from a spoon onto a hot griddle to form a backward letter. (Letters need to be reversed like this to appear right when the pancake letters are served.) When the letter is brown on the bottom, pour ¼ cup of batter over the letter. When bubbles form on top, turn.

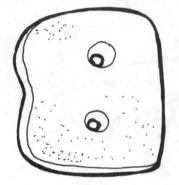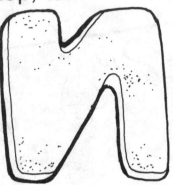

Pancake Messages:

Trace around a round object or make a large circle with a compass. Write a pancake message like this one to a friend.

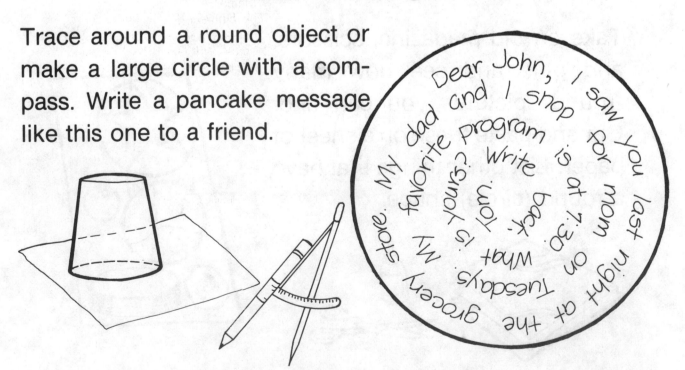

Dear John, I saw you last night at the grocery store. My dad and I shop for mom on Tuesdays. My favorite program is at 7:30. Write back. What is yours?
Tom

From *Recipes for Learning* by Gail Lewis and Jean M. Shaw, ©1979 by Goodyear Publishing Company, Inc.

Breads without an oven:

A picture recipe:

Crack 6 eggs and beat. Mix in a large bowl.

Add 1 CUP milk and 1 CUP cream.

Mix with a spoon. Add 1 CUP 1 CUP flour.

1 teaspoon salt and 2 tablespoons

melted margarine. Cook on hot skillet.

Money

Add up what it will cost to make flapjacks if you have to buy all the ingredients. Use the price list below.

1 dozen eggs	=	$ .79
1 quart milk	=	.89
1 pint cream	=	.57
2 pounds flour	=	.50
1 box salt	=	.20
1 pound margarine	=	.49
Total		$

Something to do at home: Find out what these ingredients cost at your grocery.

91

From *Recipes for Learning* by Gail Lewis and Jean M. Shaw, ©1979 by Goodyear Publishing Company, Inc.

A picture recipe in metrics

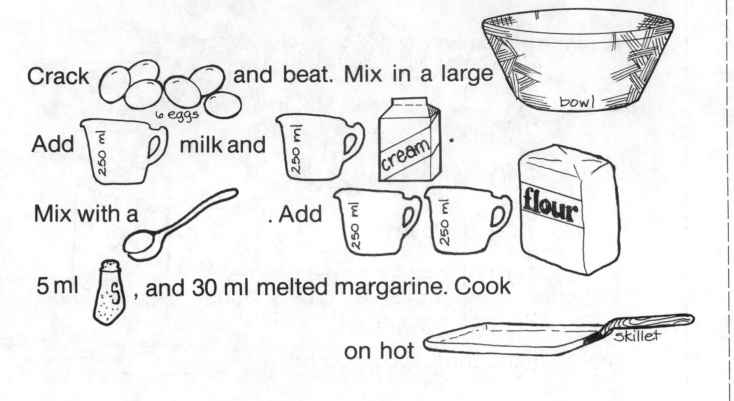

Crack [6 eggs] and beat. Mix in a large bowl.

Add [250 ml] milk and [250 ml] cream.

Mix with a [spoon]. Add [250 ml] [250 ml] flour.

5 ml [salt], and 30 ml melted margarine. Cook

on hot skillet.

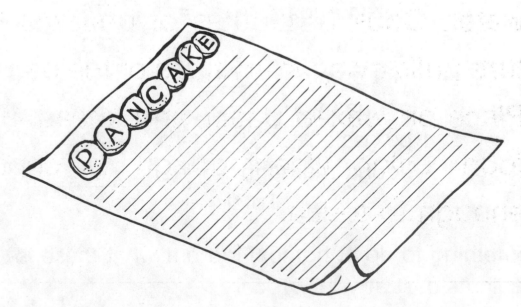

Use the letters in PANCAKE and
make as many new words as you
can. Use a piece of notebook paper.

From *Recipes for Learning* by Gail Lewis and Jean M. Shaw, ©1979 by Goodyear Publishing Company, Inc.

Play Dough

250 ml flour

250 ml water

125 ml salt

10 ml cream of tartar

30 ml salad oil

Food coloring

Mix dry ingredients. Add oil and water. Cook 3 minutes or until mixture pulls away from sides of the pan. Place on waxed paper and knead in food color when dough is cool enough to touch.

93

Play Dough

1 c. flour

1 c. water

½ c. salt

2 t. cream of tartar

2 T. salad oil

Food coloring

Mix dry ingredients. Add oil and water. Cook 3 minutes or until mixture pulls away from sides of pan. Place on waxed paper and knead in food color when dough is cool enough to touch.

From *Recipes for Learning* by Gail Lewis and Jean M. Shaw, ©1979 by Goodyear Publishing Company, Inc.

Shopping List

- Flour
- Salt
- Cream of tartar
- Cooking oil
- Food color

Equipment List

- Hot plate or stove
- Medium saucepan
- Hot pads
- Waxed paper (to knead on)
- Measuring spoons
- Measuring cups
- Mixing spoons

White Ingredients

- Play dough has three white ingredients—flour, salt, and cream of tartar. Compare "grainy" salt to smooth, powdery flour and to powdery sharp-smelling cream of tartar.
- Discuss other white ingredients *(continued on back)*   PLAY DOUGH 53

Language Activities
(vocabulary builders)

Dough, dough, and more dough . . .
List and discuss as many doughs as possible. Some starters: play dough, bread dough, sour dough, cookie dough, donut dough (alliteration), pancake dough, pie dough, dough (money)

Play Dough Actions
Give each child in a small group some play dough and have them manipulate their dough. Actions are named and discussed. You may want to list the actions on a pad or chalkboard. Some possibilities: fold it, knead it, pound it, roll it, coil it, flatten it, make it into a pancake, make it into a sausage, make it into small balls, make it into an egg, punch it, make fingerprints in it, mark it with fingernails.
How many more can your class add?

PLAY DOUGH 54

Try These for Extra Fun
with Play Dough!

"Press-Ins"
Use all or some of the following to press into play dough:

- Spools
- Old pencils
- Forks
- Small rocks
- Dry sponges
- Small plastic animals
- Small blocks—leave ABC imprints or shapes
- Scraps of textured cloth—burlap, corduroy
- Small plastic or cardboard geometric figures
- Tissue rolls

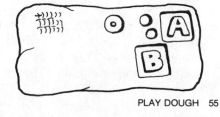

PLAY DOUGH 55

Use Your Senses

Smell homemade and commercially made play doughs. Then close your eyes and identify each by smelling. Smell other doughs—cookie, sawdust dough. Compare "nose-notes."

Look at several doughs. Talk about and list similarities and differences. Tell which are smooth, grainy, oily, etc.

Feel various doughs. Use words to describe how they feel. Close your eyes or use a blindfold. Try to match small balls of different doughs.

Measure . . . Measure . . . Measure

. . . more measurements of your play dough ingredients . . . The children measure ingredients for the recipe in milliliters, a measure of **volume**. Further explore the amounts of each ingredient by **weighing** them.
(continued on back)

PLAY DOUGH 56

95

From *Recipes for Learning* by Gail Lewis and Jean M. Shaw, ©1979 by Goodyear Publishing Company, Inc.

Observations

- Taste ingredients as you work. Cream of tartar may be mixed in water to taste. It tastes sour. Ask the children if you are using salt or sugar—taste to be sure.

- Point out solid and liquid ingredients. As it cooks, the play dough changes from liquid to solid.

- Watch steam as it rises from pan.

- Decide on a color or colors to tint the dough. Decide what colors need to be mixed. Predict results of mixing colors.

- Discuss how the children know the dough is getting hot—steam, bubbles, flame, or color of heating element may be clues.

(continued from front)
such as sugar, cornstarch, baking powder, baking soda, powdered milk, and "white" cornmeal.
- Make a list of foods that are essentially white—for example, the white meat of chicken, pears, and macaroni.
- Try to separate a grain or two of salt, flour, and cream of tartar. Which is bigger? Smaller?

More Tips

- Put drops of food color in center of each child's dough. Fold the dough over. Then have the children knead the color in.
- Work on waxed paper, foil, or oilcloth to protect the table from oil and food color.
- Explain that dough should not be tasted after it has been played with.
- Store dough in covered containers or wrap well in foil or plastic wrap.
- Cookie cutters add to fun with play dough.

(continued from front)
- Weigh the flour and the salt and compare weights.
- Weigh the water and the oil and compare weights.
- Weigh the total amount of cooked dough.
- Weigh the empty flour sack or salt box.
- Weigh a salad oil bottle full, then when empty.

Play Dough Cards

Xerox and cut out the play dough cards in Chapter 7 (pages 158-161) and cover them with clear contact paper or sheets of acetate to protect them. Have the children form play dough over the large shapes on the cards. If various colors of dough are available, encourage the children to match colors. They may have better luck covering the letter and numeral cards if they first make a "snake" of play dough and then form the "snake" around the letter or numeral outline.

"Use-Withs"
These are fun to use with play dough:
- Old scissors—cut strips of "noodles"
- Rolling pins or plastic glasses to use for rolling
- Dull knives or tongue depressors to cut dough with
- Old pencils to press in and roll with
- Styrofoam shapes to press in
- Pictures—use to suggest "foods" to make
- Containers for "foods"—berry boxes, egg cartons, meat trays, etc.
- Play dishes and pans
- Be sure to use play dough in the "store" or "house" in your room
- Squash bits of play dough through a garlic press to make skinny strands of "hair" for heads, beards, or other embellishments for play dough creatures

96

Popcorn

You will need:

  popcorn

  vegetable oil

  salt

  popcorn popper

  or pan with lid

Pour in enough oil to cover bottom of popper. Put two kernels of corn in oil. Cover popper with lid. When the two kernels pop, the oil is hot enough to add the rest of the corn (175 ml of popcorn kernels will make 2 liters of popped corn.)

From *Recipes for Learning* by Gail Lewis and Jean M. Shaw, ©1979 by Goodyear Publishing Company, Inc.

Popcorn

You will need:

    popcorn

    vegetable oil

    salt

    popcorn popper

    or pan with lid

Pour in enough oil to cover bottom of popper. Put two kernels of corn in oil. Cover popper with lid. When the two kernels pop, the oil is hot enough to add the rest of the corn. (¾ c. of popcorn kernels will make 2 qts. popped corn.)

From *Recipes for Learning* by Gail Lewis and Jean M. Shaw, ©1979 by Goodyear Publishing Company, Inc.

Equipment List

- Popcorn popper or hot plate and large pan with lid
- Saucepan
- Spoon
- Potato peeler

Shopping List

- Vegetable oil
- Popcorn
- Margarine
- Dried apples ●
- Apple spice, pumpkin spice, or cinnamon ●
- Flavored gelatin ✳
- Miniature marshmallows ✳
- Brown sugar

Key:
● for apple popcorn only
✳ for Jell-O popcorn balls only

Suggestions

Spread a large, clean white sheet on the floor. Put a popcorn popper without its lid in the center of the sheet. Add popcorn to popper. Heat and watch the popcorn pop.

POPCORN 57

(continued on back)

Apple Popcorn

Pop 1½ cups of popcorn. This will make about 4 quarts of popped corn. Set aside in a large bowl.

Melt ½ cup margarine in a saucepan. Add 1 cup dried apples, ½ cup brown sugar, and 1 teaspoon apple spice, cinnamon, or pumpkin spice.

Cook until apples are "puffy" and beginning to brown. Pour over popped corn. Toss corn until it is evenly coated with mixture. Super good!

POPCORN 58

Jell-O Popcorn Balls

- 1 stick margarine
- 2 c. miniature marshmallows
- 1 pkg. (3 oz.) flavored gelatin
- 4 qts. popped corn

Melt margarine. Add marshmallows and stir until melted. Add gelatin and stir until mixed. Pour over popped corn. Toss until mixed well. Form into balls with buttered hands.

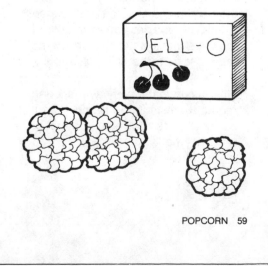

POPCORN 59

Cheesy Corn

MIX:
  1 c. grated cheese
  ½ c. melted margarine
  1 t. salt
POUR:
  over 4 qts. popped corn
TOSS:
  until popcorn and cheese mixture are mixed

A Cheese-Tasting Party!

Bring several kinds of cheese to school and cut them into small cubes so that the children can taste and talk about each kind. The children could volunteer to bring cheese, or you could take a trip to the local grocery or delicatessen.

POPCORN 60

From *Recipes for Learning* by Gail Lewis and Jean M. Shaw, ©1979 by Goodyear Publishing Company, Inc.

Dried Apples

Have the children peel a few apples with a potato peeler and remove the cores with an apple corer. Cut the apples into slices—there will be a hole in the center. String and hang the slices in the window. Have the children watch them change over a period of time.

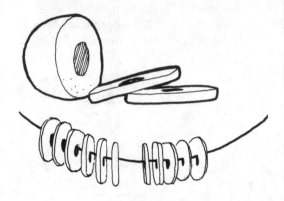

(continued from front)

- Encourage the children to talk about good safety habits when using popcorn poppers, hot plates, and other dangerous kitchen equipment.

- Put several kernels of popcorn in the popper with oil. Replace the lid and observe the movement of the kernel before it pops.

- Have the children work with doubling and halving the recipes.

- List other foods that contain starch.

- Talk about how each sense is affected when the popcorn is popped: smell, sight, taste, hearing.

- Let each child pretend to be a popcorn kernel. When you clap your hands, they pop!

- Use the lined recipe chart for other popcorn recipes: Apple Popcorn, Cheesy Corn, Jell-O Popcorn Balls.

Facts to Share

- Popcorn kernels have a thick, tough skin. Each kernel has a little water and starch in it. When the kernel gets hot, the water turns to steam.
- When the steam expands, the kernel explodes and you see the white starch.
- Buy colored popcorn kernels and use them for color and classification activities.

Estimation
(to use with Jell-O Popcorn Balls)

- How many marshmallows will one cup hold?

- Fill a measuring cup with miniature marshmallows. Put the cup at the cooking center with a sign, paper, and pencil. Leave it there until all the children have had a chance to estimate the number and record their estimates on a sheet of paper. After everyone has had a turn, count the marshmallows to see who came the closest to the correct amount.

- Fill the cup to the halfway mark and repeat the estimation game. Was it easier to guess correctly the first or second time?

Pellon* Popcorn

Using the outline on the back of this card, make pellon popcorn to use for a flannel-board drill. These can be used for making sets, counting, etc. Numerals, words, and letters can be added with magic marker for other drills.

* Pellon is an interfacing; it is found in fabric stores.

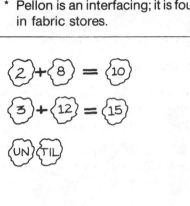

Area Estimation

Have the children use popped or unpopped kernels of popcorn to work the worksheet on area estimation in Chapter 7 (page 186). Prior to this activity, you may want to do the following as a large-group activity.

A. "How many reading books will it take to cover *child's name* 's desk?"
B. "How many children can stand on this newspaper?"

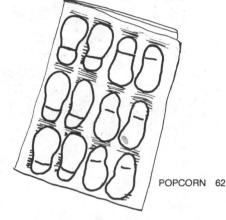

IDEAS for "Cut-Outs" Sheet

1. Let the children take each popcorn recipe card and match the cut-out ingredients to them.
2. Put the cutouts in alphabetical order. Write the words on a separate sheet in alphabetical order.
3. Find ways to classify ingredients (Examples: solid, liquid, granular).
4. Take the sheet to the store (or use ads) and find the prices.
5. Use play money to buy and sell the cut-out ingredients.
6. Make up a "pretend" recipe using some or all of the cut-out ingredients. Write the recipe and use the cutouts for rebus pictures.

For "cutouts" sheets, see Chapter 7, page 162.

"Metrics"

Let the children use a measuring cup and spoons that are marked with both metric and standard measures, and decide on the approximate metric measurements for Cheesy Corn, Jell-O Popcorn Balls, and Apple Popcorn.

POPCORN

Creative Movement

1. Be a kernel of popcorn
   A. In a jar or bag . . .
   B. In a popper . . .
   C. Being eaten . . .

2. Be a stick of margarine
   A. In the refrigerator . . .
   B. In a saucepan on a stove . . .

3. Be yourself walking in melted marshmallows!

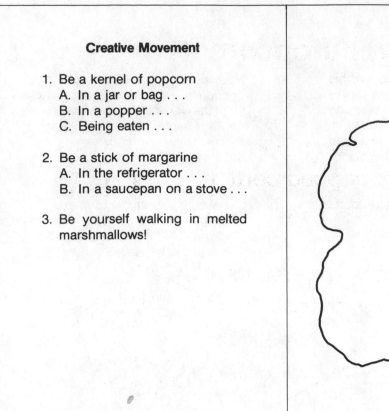

The "Not for Cooking" Cookbook

Have each child dictate or write a pretend recipe for anything he or she wishes. Type or copy these on a spirit master and make copies for each child to take home and read.

102

From *Recipes for Learning* by Gail Lewis and Jean M. Shaw, ©1979 by Goodyear Publishing Company, Inc.

Dyed Popcorn #1

Fill three paper cups with water.
Add food coloring to each cup.
Add five kernels of popped corn to each cup. Stir once and quickly remove.
Place dyed popcorn on paper towels or newspaper to dry.
(Do not eat!)

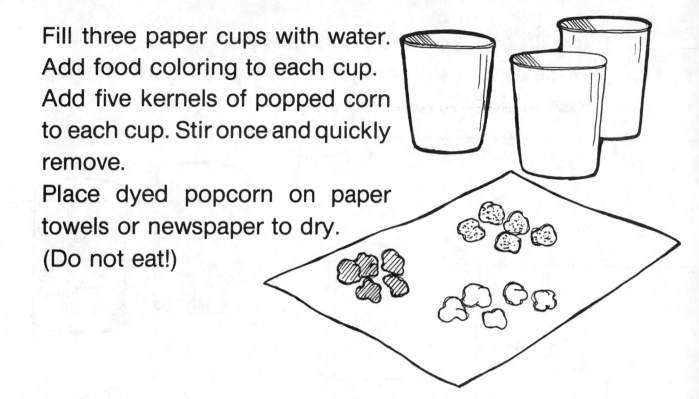

Things to do with Dyed Popcorn

1. Make your name.
2. Make a collage.
3. Make numerals or letters.
4. Make a popcorn picture.
5. Make a popcorn construction.

You will need paper or cardboard, glue, and popped dyed popcorn.

103

From *Recipes for Learning* by Gail Lewis and Jean M. Shaw, ©1979 by Goodyear Publishing Company, Inc.

Dyed Popcorn #2

Fill a small bag ½ full with popped corn.
Put several "shakes" of powdered paint in bag.
Close tightly and shake.
(Do not eat!)

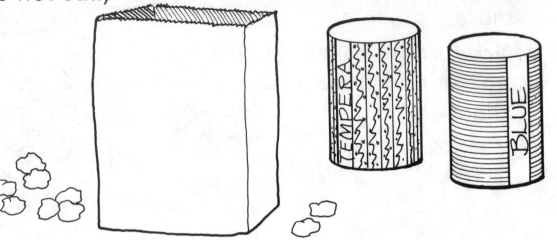

Strategy — for 2

Materials needed: unpopped corn kernels.

Procedure: Arrange any number of kernels in three rows. Two players take turns removing any number of kernels from one row only. You have to remove at least one, but you may take as many as the whole row. The player who takes the last kernel wins.

104

VEGETABLE STEW

Cooked soup bones

Many varieties of vegetables

1 Pkg. onion-soup mix

Salt

Cooking pot

Wash vegetables carefully and cut into pieces. Make a variety of shapes and sizes—chunks, "coins," bias-cut strips, sticks, and others. Decide which vegetables must be cooked the longest (potatoes, beets, carrots). Put these in first. Add soup mix. Add other vegetables. Cook until vegetables are tender. Add salt to taste.

105

From *Recipes for Learning* by Gail Lewis and Jean M. Shaw, ©1979 by Goodyear Publishing Company, Inc.

Vege-Riddles

Teacher or children read the riddles. Take turns answering them. Match vegetables in Chapter 7 (page 163) or word cards with riddles. Make riddles of your own in the spaces at the bottom.

What am I?
- I grow in the dark, but I have eyes!
- I help you to see in the dark.
- Lots of us grow together in a pod.
- You can eat my stalks and leaves.
- I'm fat and red and go into catsup.
- You can eat my white flowers raw.
- I can make you cry with my smell.
- I'm fat and purple-red.
- We come in yellow, green, white, brown, or red.
- You can pop me or eat me from a cob.

Make your own riddles here.

_____

_____

_____

_____

_____

From *Recipes for Learning* by Gail Lewis and Jean M. Shaw, ©1979 by Goodyear Publishing Company, Inc.

Shopping List

- A variety of vegetables
- Soup bones (¾ to 2 lbs.)
- Onion-soup mix
- Salt

Equipment List

- Electric cooking pot or, if using a stove, a large pot with lid
- Stirring spoons
- Knives
- Vegetable peeler
- Cutting board
- Bowls and spoons for eating

Friendship Stew

Have each child contribute a vegetable for the stew, and share the results.

Vege-Math

Weighing Vegetables

Estimate the weights of various vegetables and test these estimates by weighing, or use a balance scale to try and get equal weights (when the pans balance) with different vegetables. If the vegetables are put into paper bags for estimating, it adds mystery to the activity. Or guess how many of each vegetable will make a pound or kilogram.

Graphing Vegetables

Make a picture or bar graph of the vegetables used in the stew or of other vegetables brought in by the children. Or let the children vote for their favorite vegetables and record the results.

Measure Vegetables

How "tall" is a carrot? How "fat" is a tomato? Let's find out . . . Have the children arrange vegetables in order (before washing and cooking) from shortest to tallest. Use a metric tape measure (from a fabric store) to measure the height of each in centimeters. Now predict the "fatness" (circumference) of each. Measure around each vegetable in centimeters.

More Help for the Teacher

Helpful Hints

- Cook the soup bones ahead of time. This is easily done by baking and browning them for about an hour. Pour off grease.

- Making stew is a good way to introduce children to a variety of vegetables. Encourage them to taste all vegetables, raw and cooked.

- Allow plenty of time to wash and chop the vegetables. Stew usually takes at least an hour to cook. In a crock pot, it can be cooked on "low" overnight.

- Vegetables might be brought from home, one per child, or purchased on a trip to the store.
(continued on back)

Many Mini Vege-Facts

Tomatoes . . . are grown by many home gardeners. They grow well in sandy soil. These juicy red giants are really fruits. We usually eat them skin, seeds, and all. Tomatoes are used in soups, stews, sauces, and catsup. They are a good source of vitamin C.

Carrots . . . are famous as "rabbit food," but boys and girls like them too. Crunchy carrots are rich in vitamin A and help to prevent night blindness. They grow underground.

Onions . . . are noted for their strong smell. Some onions, such as large purple ones, are actually quite mild. Onions grow in layers that fall apart into rings as they are cut up. Onions have shallow roots. They may be cooked many ways.

From *Recipes for Learning* by Gail Lewis and Jean M. Shaw, ©1979 by Goodyear Publishing Company, Inc.

Lucy Rabbit Song

Dramatize the song. Let one or two children come to the center of the song circle and pretend to eat vegetables while the other children sing and shoo the rabbits away. Other children then go to the center for another verse. Vary the names of vegetables—use some unusual ones, such as collards, parsnips, parsley, and turnips.

Lu-cy Rab-bit Hey! Hey!

In my gar-den Hey! Hey!

Eat my Car-rots Hey! Hey!

All night long — Hey! Hey!

Shoo rab-bit 'way Hey! Hey!

SHOO! (loudly spoken)

Stew and Soup Stories

Many stories use the theme of adding ingredients to a virtually empty pot and ending up with a delicious soup or stew. Some are:

The Turnip — a Russian folk tale retold by Alexei Tolstoi
Stone Soup written and illustrated by Marcia Brown
Nail Soup by Harve Zemach

Other vegetable-related stories are:

Spoiled Tomatoes by Bill Martin. This book deals with the problem of spoiling foods
Dragon Stew by T. McGowen
Plants That Feed the World by Rose Frisch

More Mini Vege-Facts

Potatoes . . . are eaten all over the world by both animals and people. They are grown from "eyes" rather than seeds. Americans eat them many ways—fried, baked, French-fried, mashed, chips. They are a good source of vitamin C.

Beans, Beans, Beans . . . they are eaten fresh, dried, canned, and frozen. Some beans are high in protein. Their plants help to enrich the soil. Green beans, yellow beans, pinto, lima . . . can you name more?

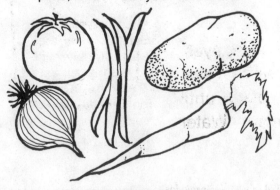

(continued from front)

Observations, Questions

• Talk about the similarities and differences among vegetables as you work.

• Notice which vegetables are juicy, starchy, crunchy, mushy, crisp, firm. Have the children suggest other descriptive words.

• Talk about where vegetables grow—underground, above ground, etc. Many may be grown locally, others shipped in.

• Talk about which vegetables are also sold frozen or canned.

• Talk about "yummy" and "yucky" vegetables and other foods.

From *Recipes for Learning* by Gail Lewis and Jean M. Shaw, ©1979 by Goodyear Publishing Company, Inc.

A Vegetable Poem

Read the poem. Do one of these:
Copy one poem in your best writing;
Write your own vege-poem; Draw a picture.

Moles Dig 'Em
Sweet potatoes, white potatoes,
Kohlrabi too.
Onions, rutabaga
To name a few.
Many yummy vegetables
Fit for a queen or king.
Little moles enjoy them all.
They'll eat 'most anything.
Vegetables.
Moles dig 'em.   Do you?

Do-It-Yourself Science

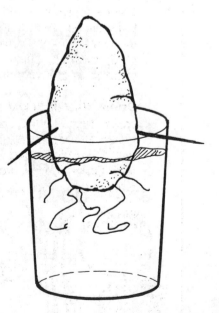

- Grow vegetables in your classroom or at home. Sweet potatoes, onions, carrots, and turnips grow well in water. Support each vegetable (with toothpicks) in a container of water. If you choose a transparent container. You'll be able to see the roots. Keep in a warm, light place. When roots appear, plants may be transferred to dirt. Good luck with vegetable growing!

- Potato Planter. White potatoes grow from eyes. Cut a potato into several parts, each with an eye. Put in damp soil. Leave in a dark place until leaves appear. Then put plants in the sun. Water well.

109

Another Vege-Poem

Read the poem. Make your own list of rhyming words.
Decide which things you like best on your list.
Draw your own picture of two or more things that rhyme.

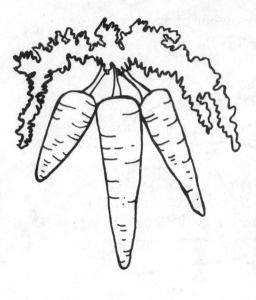

Carrots

Buy 'em, eat 'em
By the bunch.
Carrots, carrots!
Crunch, crunch, crunch.
Crisp round carrots
Orange and gold.
Full of vitamins,
I'm told.

Crazy-Mixed-Up Plant Baskets

This time use a turnip, carrot, or sweet potato. Cut off a bit of the root end and hollow out the vegetable. Poke in 3 or 4 toothpicks as shown. Hang the vegetable stem side down. Put water in the hollow hole. Watch it grow. Surprise! Leaves grow **up**! Keep it in a sunny place. Water well.

110

...Pure Corn...

Read the jokes • Learn them • Share them

"What has 20 eyes but still can't see?"
"A potato!"

"Why is a potato never cold?"
"Because it has a jacket!!"

"Where did the baby ear of corn come from?"
"The stalk brought him."

Lettuce unite!

"How many peas are in a pint?"
"Just one! Pint begins with p!"

We want our just dessert!

"When does an Irish potato lose its nationality?"
"When it becomes a French Fry!"

In the great Cabbage-Tomato race, the cabbage was ahead, but the tomato was trying to ketchup!

Find more jokes. Write them here.

_____

_____

_____

_____

_____

_____

_____

_____

From *Recipes for Learning* by Gail Lewis and Jean M. Shaw, ©1979 by Goodyear Publishing Company, Inc.

More Vege-Riddles

1. Many eyes have I, but I can't see. What am I?
2. Put me in a pie, or eat me mashed; you might also call me a yam! What am I?
3. I rhyme with potato, but I have seeds inside. What am I?
4. I get chopped and am eaten on your hamburger. What am I?
5. Guess me. I'm green and rhyme with sea.
6. Bugs Bunny loves me. I'm a . . .

1. potato   2. sweet potato   3. tomato   4. onion   5. pea   6. carrot

Make More Vege-Riddles

_____

_____

_____

_____

_____

_____

Share your riddles with your friends.

From *Recipes for Learning* by Gail Lewis and Jean M. Shaw, ©1979 by Goodyear Publishing Company, Inc.

Vegetable Art

Vegetable Prints
Cut leftover vegetables (or fruits) so that a textured surface is exposed. Prepare a paint pad: put tempera paint onto a sponge or paper towel in a pan. Dip the vegetables into the paint—just a little paint is needed. Print onto paper. Try onions, peppers, corn, lemons, cabbage.

Creative Movement

Vegetables remind us of many shapes, postions, and sizes. Explore some of these with your body. Try these with your friends:

• Arrange yourselves like peas in a pod.

• Lie still like a fat potato underground.

• Show how you eat corn on a cob.

• Pretend you're a fat, juicy tomato. Uh oh! You get squished!

• Now you're a rabbit who sees a carrot.

113

From *Recipes for Learning* by Gail Lewis and Jean M. Shaw, ©1979 by Goodyear Publishing Company, Inc.

Potato Prints

Cut a potato in half. Cut a pattern, letter, numeral into it.
Or sketch a shape, then cut away the background.
Dip potato into paint. Print onto paper.

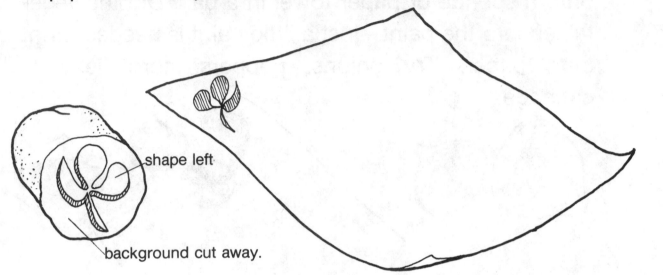

shape left

background cut away.

Potato Games . . . Try Them

Hot Potato

Pass a real potato or ball around a circle of friends. Play or sing a song as each player tries to pass the potato fast because it's "hot." Stop the music. The player who holds the potato now becomes the one to stop the music. Keep that hot potato going!

One Potato, Two Potato

Try the rhyme below to help you choose or take turns:

One potato, two potato,
three potato, four.
Five potato, six potato,
seven potato, MORE!

The word "more" marks the choice. Use this instead of "Eeny, meeny, miny, mo."

114

Oven or Toaster-Oven Recipes

"CRUNCHY" GRANOLA

Mix together in a large bowl:

☐ 750 ml rolled oats

△ 250 ml shredded coconut

○ 175 ml wheat germ

◇ 175 ml chopped nuts

▭ 175 ml soy beans

☆ 125 ml sunflower seeds

⏢ 75 ml cooking oil

⬡ 75 ml honey

⬭ 3 ml each of vanilla and salt

Bake in flat pan at 150° C (300° F.) until crisp and crunchy. Stir often.

From *Recipes for Learning* by Gail Lewis and Jean M. Shaw, ©1979 by Goodyear Publishing Company, Inc.

"CRUNCHY" GRANOLA

Mix together in a large bowl:

☐ 3 c. rolled oats

△ 1 c. shredded coconut

○ ¾ c. wheat germ

◇ ¾ c. chopped nuts

▭ ¾ c. soy beans

☆ ½ c. sunflower seeds

⏢ ⅓ c. cooking oil

⬡ ⅓ c. honey

◯ ½ t. each of vanilla and salt

Bake in flat pan at 300° F. until crisp and crunchy. Stir often.

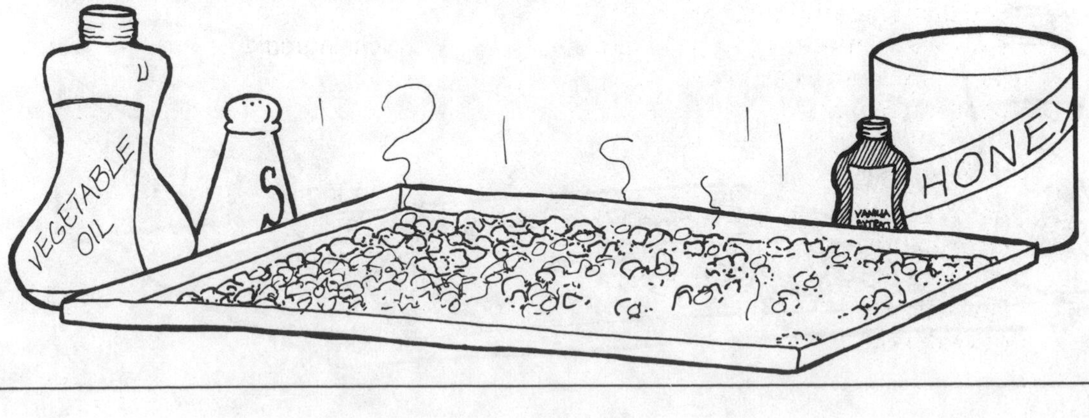

From *Recipes for Learning* by Gail Lewis and Jean M. Shaw, ©1979 by Goodyear Publishing Company, Inc.

Shopping List

- Rolled oats
- Shredded coconut
- Wheatgerm
- Nuts
- Soybeans
- Sunflower seeds
- Salad oil
- Honey
- Vanilla
- Salt

Equipment List

- Mixing bowl
- Spoons
- Measuring cup, spoons
- Large, shallow baking pan

GRANOLA 69

Color-Coding Ingredients

On the recipe, each ingredient is marked with a geometric shape. Find the similar shapes in Chapter 7 (page 165). Color the shapes on the recipe and on the cutout page—for example, use yellow for squares, orange for triangles, blue for circles, etc. Then cut out the symbols and paste or glue them to the appropriate ingredients. Have the children match symbols and ingredients as they prepare the recipe.

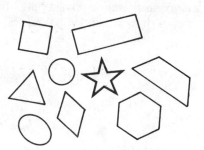

GRANOLA 70

A Sharing Theme

There are many things the children can do to add to a sharing theme as they prepare the granola recipe. Some suggestions:

- Have the children bring in different ingredients for the recipe. Emphasize that it takes contributions from many persons to make the entire recipe.

- Let small groups research the origins of the various ingredients and then share the information with the class. On a map, show where the ingredients are grown. Many parts of the world have "shared" their bounty to enable the class to make the recipe.

- Make an extra batch of granola to share with another class, or with a group of old people. Wrap granola in plastic wrap, then top it off with a colorful bow.

GRANOLA 71

Similarities and Differences

As you work with the various granola ingredients, help the children make careful observations about similarities and differences in them. Some suggestions:

- Which ingredients are the same color? Which are different colors?

- Which ingredients are flat? Wavy? Round?

- Which ingredients are liquid? Dry?

- Which ingredients are less than 1 cm long? Are any more than 1 cm long? Are any ingredients less than 1 mm long?

- Which ingredients can be crushed into smaller pieces with a spoon? Which cannot?

(continued on back)

GRANOLA 72

119

From *Recipes for Learning* by Gail Lewis and Jean M. Shaw, ©1979 by Goodyear Publishing Company, Inc.

Where Do Ingredients Come From?

Have groups of students do research to find out where the various ingredients are grown. If any are grown locally, arrange to visit the site, if possible, to learn more about the process.

The cooking oil used in the granola may be soybean oil or corn oil. If either soybeans or corn are grown locally, find out more about how they are planted and grown. Also assign students to investigate the process of extracting vegetable oils.

Mystery Bags

Put small amounts of ingredients into paper bags and let children guess the contents by various methods—smelling, listening as the bags are shaken, feeling the weight of the bags, or touching the contents to feel the texture. Make a bag of clues about the ingredients. Draw out clues, read them and then guess.

(continued from front)

- Which ingredients are vegetable products? Which are not?

- Which ingredients grow above the ground? Below the ground?

- Which are animal products?

- Which ingredients are sweet? Salty? Sour?

From *Recipes for Learning* by Gail Lewis and Jean M. Shaw, ©1979 by Goodyear Publishing Company, Inc.

Metric Measures

Fool a Friend
Find two small opaque containers (boxes, film cans). Fill them with two different granola ingredients. Ask a friend which is heavier. Estimate weights. Verify by measuring on a scale.

Just a Pinch
Try to "pinch" up 5 ml of dry oatmeal. See how close you have come by measuring. Now try to "pinch" up just 1 ml of oatmeal.

Texture Pictures

Use one or more granola ingredients to make a texture picture. Put glue on cardboard or sturdy paper. Sprinkle or place ingredients on areas. Outline areas with yarn if desired.

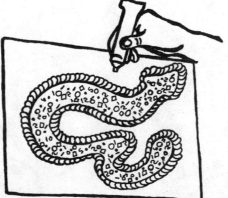

121

From *Recipes for Learning* by Gail Lewis and Jean M. Shaw, ©1979 by Goodyear Publishing Company, Inc.

Metric Areas

Measure each rectangle below in centimeters. Figure out each area in square centimeters. Predict how many pieces of oatmeal or soybean will fit on the area. Check your estimate.

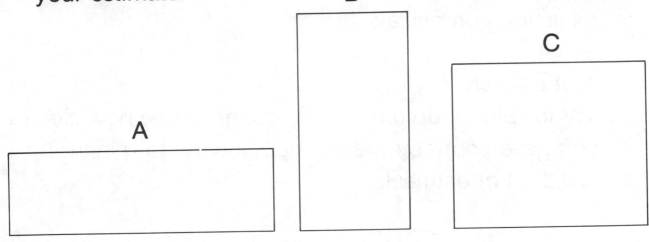

Nutshell Art

Glue paper and yarn to pecan shells. Make features with marker.

Make TINY BOATS from walnut halves. Attach a tiny sail made of a toothpick and paper. Stick it in a wad of clay.

122

From *Recipes for Learning* by Gail Lewis and Jean M. Shaw, ©1979 by Goodyear Publishing Company, Inc.

Alphabet Pretzels

Dissolve in a large bowl:

    125 ml water

    1 pkg. (7 g) yeast

Mix: 1000 ml flour

    15 ml sugar

Beat in a small bowl and set aside:

    1 egg

    5 ml water

Mix yeast mixture with 750 ml of the flour-sugar mixture. Knead mixture and work in 250 ml flour. Divide dough into 20 to 30 pieces. Shape into letters. Paint with egg mixture. Sprinkle with salt. Bake 25 minutes at 230° C (450° F.).

123

From *Recipes for Learning* by Gail Lewis and Jean M. Shaw, ©1979 by Goodyear Publishing Company, Inc.

Alphabet Pretzels

Dissolve in a large bowl:

    ½ c. water

    1 pkg. yeast

Mix: 4 c. flour

    1 T. sugar

Beat in a small bowl and set aside:

    1 egg

    1 t. water

Mix yeast mixture with 3 cups of the flour-sugar mixture. Knead mixture and work in 1 cup flour. Divide dough into 20 to 30 pieces. Shape into letters. Paint with egg mixture. Sprinkle with salt. Bake 25 minutes at 450° F.

124

Shopping List

- Yeast
- Flour
- Sugar
- Salt
- Egg

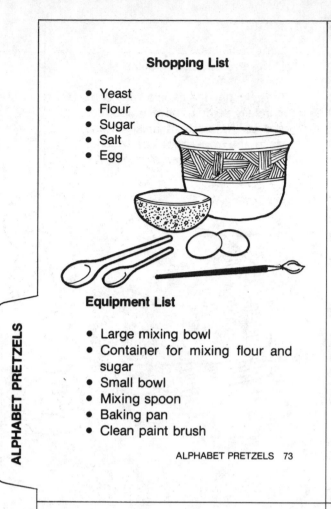

Equipment List

- Large mixing bowl
- Container for mixing flour and sugar
- Small bowl
- Mixing spoon
- Baking pan
- Clean paint brush

Helpful Hints

- Have the children roll dough into a long "snake" first, and then form into various letters of the alphabet.

- Have letters near the cooking center to use as models for forming letters.

- Leave a few pretzels unglazed (with egg) and unsalted for taste comparisons.

- Make alphabet letters out of salt dough and play dough too.

Using Pretzels

Do an activity or two with the pretzels before eating them. Or make an extra batch to use in games such as those below or on the back.

The children hold one pretzel each and:

- Arrange themselves in alphabetical order.

- Name words that begin with the letter.

- Arrange themselves according to the shape of the letter—round, straight, combinations.

Mold-a-Length

Ask the children to try to mold a pretzel exactly 1 decimeter long. Now check by measuring. Try to mold pretzels of lengths such as 8 cm, 2 cm, 5 cm. You can also ask the children to guess the length of broken-off cooked pretzels. Always verify the guesses by measuring. If children are familiar with the concept of area, mold a bit of dough with area 6 cm^2, 8 cm^2, 10 cm^2, 12 cm^2. Have the children note different shapes that have the same area.

From *Recipes for Learning* by Gail Lewis and Jean M. Shaw, ©1979 by Goodyear Publishing Company, Inc.

Shapes, Shapes, Shapes!

Form pretzels into many shapes to reinforce concepts taught in various units and areas. For example:
Numerals
Geometric shapes
Seasonal shapes such as
eggs   hearts
pumpkins   trees
Descriptive words
zigzags, coils, balls

Pretzel "Log" Cabins

To make tiny log cabins, glue commercially made or homemade pretzels to the sides of milk cartons. Make the roof from construction paper. Add a paper chimney and tiny paper people.

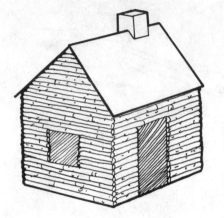

Pick-a-Pretzel Game

Find the Pick-a-Pretzel game in Chapter 7 (page 166). Color the pretzels, if desired. Laminate the pieces or cover them with clear contact paper. Cut out the pieces. Attach "box" to an old cereal box, shoe box, or sack. Take turns drawing pretzels from the box. Name the letters, name a word beginning with the letters drawn, or play the directions game on the back of the pretzels. You can also write words on the pretzels for the children to read.

The Form-a-Word Game

The teacher or a child holds a word card and the children who have pretzel letters from the word arrange themselves (and their pretzels) so that they spell the word.

Match pretzels to pictures
- of words
- of objects whose name begins with that letter

The Guess-Who Game

Hold up pretzels to form the initials of famous persons—or class members. Give clues as to the identity.

126

Pretzel Word Hunt

Divide some friends or your work group into teams. Give each team a "pretzel" word or phrase. Find as many little words as possible in the word or phrase. If you work on the board it is easy to check and compare. Some starters:

- Salty pretzels (some words: salt, tall, are, tall, see)

- Pretzel letters (let, tree, see, letter, seep, tee)

- Flour, sugar, salt (for, sat, fat, log, fur at, or)

Find Out . . .

how pretzels are made in a factory. Write to a pretzel-maker and ask for information. Perhaps you could also arrange for a visit. Share the information you find with the class.

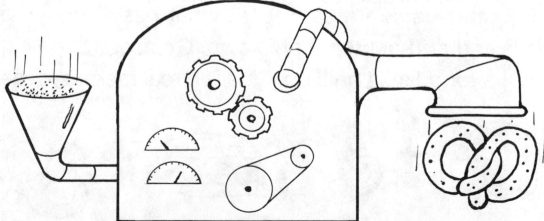

127

From *Recipes for Learning* by Gail Lewis and Jean M. Shaw, ©1979 by Goodyear Publishing Company, Inc.

Pass a Pink Pretzel

Make phrases or sentences with "p" words. List these on the chalkboard or on paper. One team can do a phrase, then "pass" the task to another team. Suggestions:

- Pass a pretzel to a pink porpoise.
- Pass a pink pretzel in a pan.
- Paul pouted passing pretzels.

"On the Picnic, I'll Bring a Pretzel. . ."

Sit in a circle. The first person says, "On the picnic, I'll bring a pretzel." The second persons says, "On the picnic, I'll bring a pretzel and a peanut butter sandwich." The third person must repeat what has already been said and add an item of his own. Go around the circle until a long list is built up. This is a real memory teaser!

From *Recipes for Learning* by Gail Lewis and Jean M. Shaw, ©1979 by Goodyear Publishing Company, Inc.

Shrink-a-Shape

Materials needed:

1. Brittle plastic, meat trays, styrofoam egg cartons, or commercial shrink-art kit

2. Portable oven or school oven

3. Permanent felt-tip markers

4. Scissors, hole punch

Directions:

Color and cut any desired shape or object from plastic or styrofoam. Put on cookie sheet or aluminum foil and place in oven. Bake at about 250° F. (120° C). Object will shrink to about 1/3 its original size and get about 9 times thicker.

129

From *Recipes for Learning* by Gail Lewis and Jean M. Shaw, ©1979 by Goodyear Publishing Company, Inc.

NAME PLATES

Use a round plastic lid, or cut a large circle from plastic or styrofoam. Decorate it with your name and something that is special to you (a pet, hobby, flower, etc.). Punch a hole in the top. Shrink it. Use on the door of your room, locker, etc.

Equipment and Materials

- Scissors
- Felt-tip markers
- Portable oven
- Styrofoam meat trays and egg cartons
- Brittle clear-plastic lids, tops, etc.

Sources of Plastic

- Disposable glasses
- Covers for cream pies, graham-cracker crusts, etc.
- Lids from cartons of potato salad, pimento cheese, etc.

Oven temperatures vary, so you might want to experiment to find the best setting to shrink your shapes. Usually 250° F. (120° C) works the best. If the oven door has a window in it, the children will enjoy watching

(continued on back)

Texture Rubs

Place completed Shrink-a-Shape on a table in a design. Cover the shapes with a piece of drawing paper. Use the side of a crayon and rub over the paper until all the shapes appear on the paper.

A Rebus Story

Have the children illustrate a story by drawing figures or objects in the story. They can copy the story on a chart and insert the figures and objects instead of some words.

(Example: Once there was a . . .)

Suggested Uses for Shrink-a-Shape

1. Small mobiles
2. Easter-egg trees
3. Christmas ornaments
4. Jewelry (bracelets, earrings, necklaces)

Transparent and Opaque

Use styrofoam and clear plastic to introduce these new terms. Label two boxes with these words and ask the children to store collected transparent and opaque objects in the appropriate boxes.

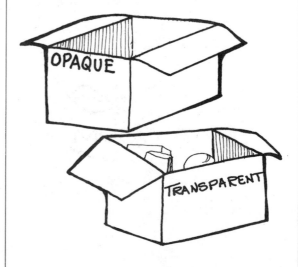

Measure Metric

Give each child a metric ruler or a strip of cardboard marked off in centimeters. Tell them the directions for making shapes with metric measurements: the children cut out each shape, shrink it, and then re-measure it to compare the difference between the original and the "shrunken" shape. They may wish to trace the original shape to use for later comparison.

(continued from front)

the "dance" their object does as it shrinks. If it folds over so much that it sticks together, the oven temperature is too hot.

If the child wishes to have a hole in the object (for necklaces, key chains, etc.), the hole should be punched before baking.

Parents' Gifts

Let the children decorate and shrink a shape for a gift key ring or chain. Punch the hole for the chain to go through before baking. These are nicer when done with clear plastic.

132

From *Recipes for Learning* by Gail Lewis and Jean M. Shaw, ©1979 by Goodyear Publishing Company, Inc.

Shrink a Glass

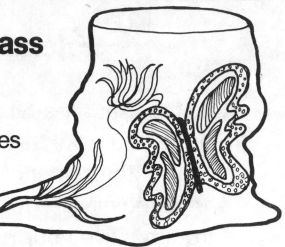

You will need:

  Clear-plastic disposable glasses
  Permanent felt-tip markers

Directions:

  Decorate a plastic glass any way you wish with the markers. (Designs work better on these than pictures.) Place the decorated glass on a cookie sheet covered with aluminum foil. Bake at about 275-300° F. (135-150° C) until it collapses.

Meat Tray Magic

You will need:

  Five meat trays (styrofoam) of the same size and shape.

Directions:

  Turn your oven to 275° F. (135° C). Place all five trays on an aluminum-foil-covered cookie sheet. As soon as they begin to shrink, remove one. Wait a few seconds and remove another. Continue doing this for number 3 and 4. Leave the last one until it is small and flat. Compare all five.

From *Recipes for Learning* by Gail Lewis and Jean M. Shaw, ©1979 by Goodyear Publishing Company, Inc.

Friendship Necklaces

Use the "Shrink-a-Glass" to make a friendship necklace. Before you bake the glass, let your teacher help punch a hole in the center of the bottom of the glass. After you shrink the glass, you can use this hole for a string to go through. Give your necklace to a friend to wear.

More Shrink Ideas!!

1. Shrink your name. Glue the letters on another meat tray for a name plaque.

2. Draw animals and people to shrink. Use these as shadow box figures, sand-box toys, gameboard markers, etc.

134

Sourdough Starter

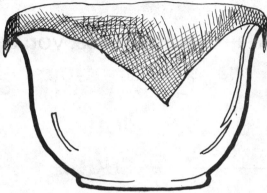

1 pkg. (7 g) dry yeast
625 ml warm water
500 ml flour
15 ml sugar

Dissolve yeast in 250 ml water. Stir in remaining water, flour, and sugar. Beat until smooth. Cover with cheesecloth, paper toweling, or plastic wrap. Let stand at room temperature five to ten days. Stir two or three times a day. (Time for mixture to ferment will depend on room temperature; if room is warm, let it stand a shorter time than if room is cool.) Cover and refrigerate until ready to use. To keep starter going, add 200 ml flour, 200 ml water, 10 ml sugar. Let stand at room temperature at least one day. Cover and refrigerate again until used.

From *Recipes for Learning* by Gail Lewis and Jean M. Shaw, ©1979 by Goodyear Publishing Company, Inc.

Sourdough Starter

1 pkg. dry yeast
2½ c. warm water
2 c. flour
1 T. sugar

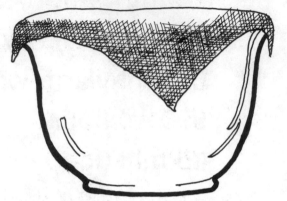

Dissolve yeast in 1 c. water. Stir in remaining water, flour, and sugar. Beat until smooth. Cover with cheesecloth, paper toweling, or plastic wrap. Let stand at room temperature five to ten days. Stir two or three times a day. (Time for mixture to ferment will depend on room temperature; if room is warm, let it stand a shorter time than if room is cool.) Cover and refrigerate until ready to use. To keep starter going, add 1 c. flour, 1 c. water, 1 t. sugar. Let stand at room temperature at least one day. Cover and refrigerate again until used.

From *Recipes for Learning* by Gail Lewis and Jean M. Shaw, ©1979 by Goodyear Publishing Company, Inc.

Sourdough Bread

1 pkg. (7 gm) dry yeast

375 ml warm water

250 ml sourdough starter

15 ml salt

15 ml sugar

1375 to 1500 ml flour

5 ml baking soda

In large bowl, soften yeast in warm water. Blend in starter, salt, and sugar. Add 625 ml flour. Beat well for five or six minutes. Cover; let rise until bubbly—about 1½ hours. Combine soda and 625 ml flour; stir into dough. Add enough additional flour to make a stiff dough. Turn out onto lightly floured board. Knead for five to seven minutes. Divide dough in half. Let rest ten minutes. Form into two loaves and place on greased baking sheet. Cut slashes on tops. Bake at 200° C (400° F.) for 35 to 40 minutes.

From *Recipes for Learning* by Gail Lewis and Jean M. Shaw, ©1979 by Goodyear Publishing Company, Inc.

Sourdough Bread

1 pkg. yeast

1½ c. warm water

1 c. sourdough starter

1 T. salt

1 T. sugar

5½ to 6 c. flour

1 t. baking soda

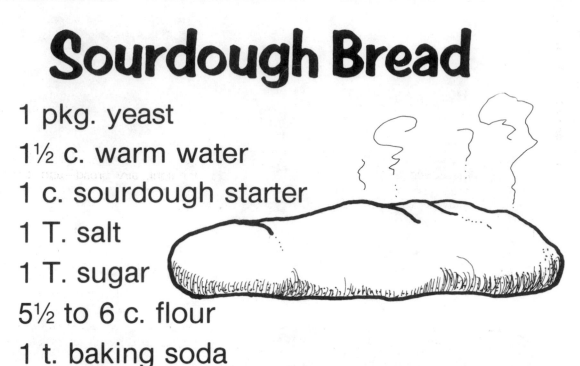

In large bowl, soften yeast in warm water. Blend in starter, sugar, and salt. Add 2½ c. flour. Beat well for five or six minutes. Cover; let rise until bubbly—about 1½ hrs. Combine soda and 2½ c. flour. Stir into dough. Add enough additional flour to make a stiff dough. Turn out onto lightly floured board. Knead for five to seven minutes. Divide dough in half. Let rest ten minutes. Form into two loaves and place on greased baking sheet. Cut slashes on tops. Bake at 400° F. for 35 to 40 minutes.

Shopping List

- Dry yeast
- Flour
- Salt
- Baking soda
- Sugar

Equipment List

- Medium bowl
- Measuring spoons
- Mixing spoons
- Baking sheet
- Hotpads
- Cheesecloth or dish towel

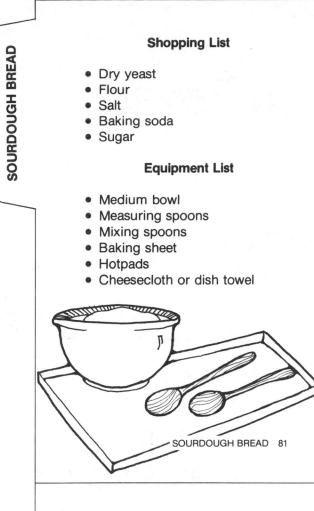

SOURDOUGH BREAD 81

The Story of Sourdough Bread

The story of sourdough bread began in the western United States in the late 1700's. Because yeast was difficult to obtain, store, and carry, and was expensive to use in every loaf of bread, settlers carried sourdough starter with them, and used it and baking soda to leaven their bread. The fermented sourdough made the bubbles necessary for light, airy bread—and it used only a small amount of yeast compared to the usual bread-making methods.

Sourdough was carried by settlers and prospectors in crock pots with tight-fitting lids. It could be mixed with flour, water, and soda and then left to rise while the settlers worked or looked for gold. More flour, water, and sugar was added to the crock each time some of the starter

(continued on back)

SOURDOUGH BREAD 82

Plan Ahead

The sourdough starter must be made five to ten days before the bread can be baked. Perhaps making the starter could be an introduction for a whole unit on grains and breads, with the baking of bread as the final activity.

Look for these . . .
notice . . . notice . . . notice

Observe the bubbles that rise with the yeast and water mixture, the starter, and the dough. How soon do they appear? Are they large or small? Do they appear near the middle, the edges, or all over?

Notice the liquid that forms on top starter. What color is it? How does it smell? Is it thick and syrupy or is it thin? Refrigerate some bread dough, and then compare its rate of rising to that of dough at room temperature.

SOURDOUGH BREAD 83

Sourdough Bread
Word Rhythms
(language activities)

Start with phrases used in bread preparation or bread names. Say the phrases or words and have the children clap the number of syllables and accents used. Let the children suggest words and phrases for clapping. Try these:
- Sourdough bread
- Mix it well
- Pumpernickle
- Russian rye bread
- White wheat bread
- Rye bread
- Dissolve the yeast
- Cornbread, cornbread
- Knead, knead, knead
- Caraway rye bread
- Batter bread
- Grease the pan

SOURDOUGH BREAD 84

139

From *Recipes for Learning* by Gail Lewis and Jean M. Shaw, ©1979 by Goodyear Publishing Company, Inc.

(continued from front)

was used. The mixture would then ferment again and be ready for another use.

Many men who traveled alone carried sourdough starter with them and made bread as a staple item in their diets. They became known as "sourdoughs." The aroma of fresh bread near a "sourdough's" fire must have been a welcome smell after a hard day of prospecting in California or Alaska. Sourdough pancakes and muffins were also made in frying pans, and were quicker to make than bread.

Many restaurants in New Orleans and San Francisco today are famous for their sourdough bread. The crusty, airy bread is served alone or with soup or stew. Kits are sold with recipes to make and pots in which to store the sourdough starter. It is also fun and easy to make from scratch.

Shapes for Sourdough Bread

Sourdough may be formed in many ways—as loaves, as muffins, or as individual pieces. Try a variety of shapes. The recipe makes two medium loaves, or is enough for 20 to 30 individual pieces. Bake smaller shapes a shorter time.

- loaf pan
- long loaf (bake on cookie sheet)
- round loaf
- rolls or individual pieces
    tiny loaves
    "snakes"
    "dots"
    figure 8's
    braids
    hearts

Alliterations: Some Silly, Some Serious

Suggest some phrases that begin with the same sound. These are alliterations. Let the children suggest others—silly or ordinary are both fun. Make a list, chart, or story. Some starters:

- Sourdough starter
- Sourdough Sam
- Silly Sourdough Sam
- Silly soup
- Salty sardine soup
- Slimy smoky salmon
- Brown Bread
- Big bumpy brown bread
- Pickled peppers
- Peppery pickled peppers
- Wild wooly western wildcats
- Big bad blue brash badger

Sourdough Adventure Game

Find this game in Chapter 7 (page 169). Xerox the gameboard and characters. Color them or let the children do it. Laminate the pieces with acetate or cover them with clear contact paper, and then cut out the pieces. Write vocabulary words, math problems, or other items on the cards. Shuffle the cards. The children take turns drawing cards and moving the characters around the gameboard.
Happy adventuring!
Strike It Rich!!

From *Recipes for Learning* by Gail Lewis and Jean M. Shaw, ©1979 by Goodyear Publishing Company, Inc.

Sourdough Sensory Experiences

You used several white powdery substances in the sourdough recipe—flour, sugar, salt, soda. Can you identify these by using your senses? Decide which is which by looking, feeling, smelling, and tasting them. Salt and sugar should be easy to separate from flour and soda by looking. Can you do it? Do the ingredients feel different? How would you describe them? Smell each ingredient—can you tell which is which? Now for a taste test: Try small samples of each on your tongue. Can you tell which parts of your tongue let you taste sweet, sour, salty, and bitter? The diagram shows the tongue areas most sensitive to many people.

Try This . . . With Yeast

Yeast is really a plant. It needs water and food to make it grow. The usual food for yeast is sugar. To enable you and your friends to watch yeast grow, set up four jars. Use ½ package of dry yeast in each. In jar #1, use yeast and ⅓ container of water. In jar #2, use yeast alone. In jar #3, use yeast, ⅓ container water and 5 ml sugar. In jar #4, use ⅓ container water and 5 ml sugar. Set all the jars in a warm place and watch the results. Of course, the well-fed yeast (in jar #3) will "grow" the best. You will see the bubbly, spongy yeast plant as it grows—the results will be fairly rapid. After 15 to 30 minutes, some bubbling will be apparent. Investigate the effects of heat and cold on yeast growth. Dissolve yeast and sugar in boiling water, ice water, and warm water. Too much heat or cold inhibits yeast growth, you will discover.

From *Recipes for Learning* by Gail Lewis and Jean M. Shaw, ©1979 by Goodyear Publishing Company, Inc.

Taste 'N' Sniff

Collect several sour substances in addition to the sourdough starter. You might start with lemon juice, vinegar, dill pickles, boric-acid water, lime juice, and grapefruit. Even sour milk will do! Smell each one. Put a little bit of each on a toothpick or cotton swab and taste it. Then decide which sour substance is the strongest. List some sour foods you like; list some you don't like. Now compare the taste and smell of sourdough starter to that of the finished bread.

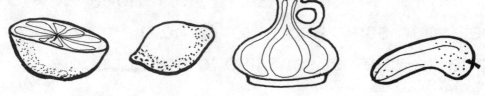

"I'll Bring the Sourdough"

With a group of friends, play the add-on sourdough game. The first player says, "When we go prospecting, I'll bring the sourdough." The second player says, "When we go prospecting, I'll bring the sourdough and the burro." Each player repeats what the ones before him have said and adds on an item. Continue taking turns until someone misses an item. Then start over again. See how many things you can take on your imaginary prospecting trip.

142

From *Recipes for Learning* by Gail Lewis and Jean M. Shaw, ©1979 by Goodyear Publishing Company, Inc.

Bread Poems . . .

Bread, Bread, Bread

White bread, wheat bread,
Pumpernickle, rye.
So many kinds of bread
For a gal or guy.

Honey, butter,
Peanut butter, jam.
So many ways to top it!
Cheese spread or ham.

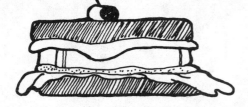

Three Ghostesses

There were three ghostesses,
Sitting on postesses,
Eating buttered toastesses,
Greasing their fistesses,
Up to their wristesses.
Oh what beastesses
To make such feastesses!

author unknown

Sourdough Science
Measure . . . Measure . . . Measure

Measure the amount of the starter and dough as they "grow" in their containers. Using a meter stick or centimeter ruler, measure the starter after mixing, after an hour, then over several days. Also measure the height of the bread dough.

STARTER

times	heights

DOUGH

times	heights

143

From *Recipes for Learning* by Gail Lewis and Jean M. Shaw, ©1979 by Goodyear Publishing Company, Inc.

Write and illustrate your own bread poem. Share your poem and picture with a friend.

Try This . . . Soda + Acid = Bubbles!

In the sourdough bread recipe, the starter is sour (acid). When soda is added to this, bubbles occur.

To see this reaction firsthand, mix some plain sourdough starter with one or two milliliters of baking soda in a glass container. Many bubbles will occur immediately.

Now vary the proportions of soda and starter. Use twice as much soda as starter. What happens? Compare that result to using twice as much starter as soda.

Also mix small equal amounts of vinegar and soda in a glass. Bubbles galore will result! Why does this happen?

Try other combinations of acid ingredients and soda. Is the reaction always the same? Does it always last the same amount of time?

144

From *Recipes for Learning* by Gail Lewis and Jean M. Shaw, ©1979 by Goodyear Publishing Company, Inc.

CHAPTER SIX

Evaluating the Cooking Program

Cooking experiences should be evaluated by both the teacher and the children. This may be done after each recipe and its related activities have been completed, and also at the end of the semester or year. The children may be asked to respond either verbally or in writing. The evaluation process will make the teacher more aware of the many learning opportunities involved in cooking experiences and help to highlight strengths and weaknesses in the learning process.

SUGGESTED QUESTIONS FOR CHILDREN

1. What is one new thing you learned from the recipe or related activities?
2. What were some new words you learned in preparing the recipe or doing the related activities?
3. Did you taste any new foods or ingredients in the recipe? If so, what?
4. Describe a change that occurred in the ingredients you used. (For example, butter melted, or gelatin hardened.)
5. What did you like best about the recipe and related activities? Why?
6. What did you like least about the recipe and related activities? Why?

SUGGESTED QUESTIONS FOR THE TEACHER

1. Did I involve every child in the recipe preparation or related activities?
2. Did I provide opportunities for practice of social learning such as sharing and cooperation?

3. Did I provide opportunities for small-muscle development as the children worked?
4. Did I take advantage of opportunities to introduce and reinforce new vocabulary words?
5. Did I capitalize on opportunities for increasing the children's measuring skills?
6. Did I increase the children's sensory awareness during the cooking and eating processes?
7. Did I turn mistakes such as spills or mismeasurements into learning experiences?
8. Were activities done in such a way as to develop the children's self-concepts?
9. Did I provide opportunities for individual children or groups of children to do independent investigations and research related to the recipe or ingredients?
10. Did I extend or modify the suggested activities to meet the needs of my group?
11. What should I change the next time we use this recipe and its related activities?
12. What should I add or delete the next time?

LOOKING AT THE COOKING PROGRAM

Use this evaluation at the end of the semester or the year.

1. Was a variety of new foods introduced during the cooking program?
2. Were different kinds of processes for preparing ingredients introduced?
3. Were cooking units introduced and culminated in a variety of ways (cooking first or last, poems, stories, art, etc.)?
4. Were similarities and differences between various recipes stressed (vocabulary words, processes, physical and chemical changes in ingredients)?
5. Were enough guidance and direction provided so that behavior problems were kept at a minimum?
6. Were time allotments sufficient so that children were neither rushed nor bored?
7. Were many different resources used so that expenditures were kept to a minimum?
8. Was some degree of parent involvement achieved?
9. What evidence of changes in children's attitudes toward learning could be attributed to cooking units?
10. What are some specific ways that cooking has enhanced and enriched the existing curriculum?
11. What are some suggestions for improving the cooking curriculum?

CHAPTER
SEVEN

Ready-to-Use
Materials

MILK

Ravenous Rabbit
Reinforcement Game

Use Ravenous Rabbit and his carrots to practice reading words, naming letters or numerals, or telling math facts.

Xerox the rabbit and carrots. Color them (or let the children do it). Glue the pages to tagboard or light cardboard. Laminate them with clear plastic or cover them with clear contact paper and then cut them out. Cut out the rabbit's mouth.

Cut the top off a half-gallon milk container or cereal box, and cut a large rectangular opening in one side of the box. Glue the rabbit to the box, matching its mouth opening to the opening in the box.

Use crayon or washable marker to write words, numbers, letters of the alphabet, etc. on the carrots. They may be wiped clean with wet or dry tissues or paper towels when you want to reuse them.

DIRECTIONS FOR CHILDREN

Read whatever is written on the carrots and then feed the carrots to the rabbit.

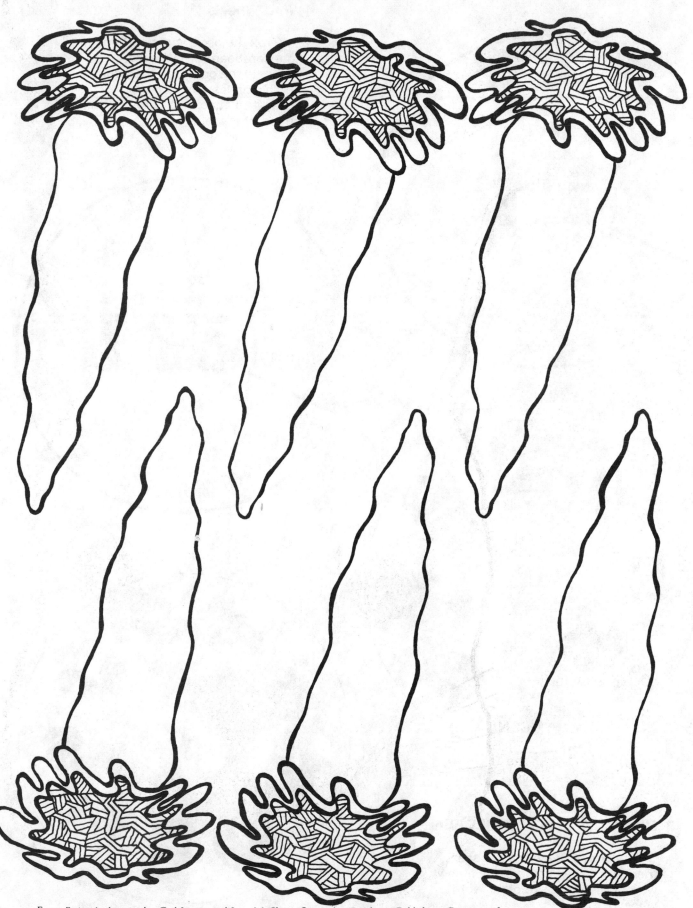

Word Wheels

Xerox the page and glue it to light cardboard or tagboard. Laminate the page and then cut out the circles. Use a paper fastener to attach the cutout wheel on top of the letter wheel.

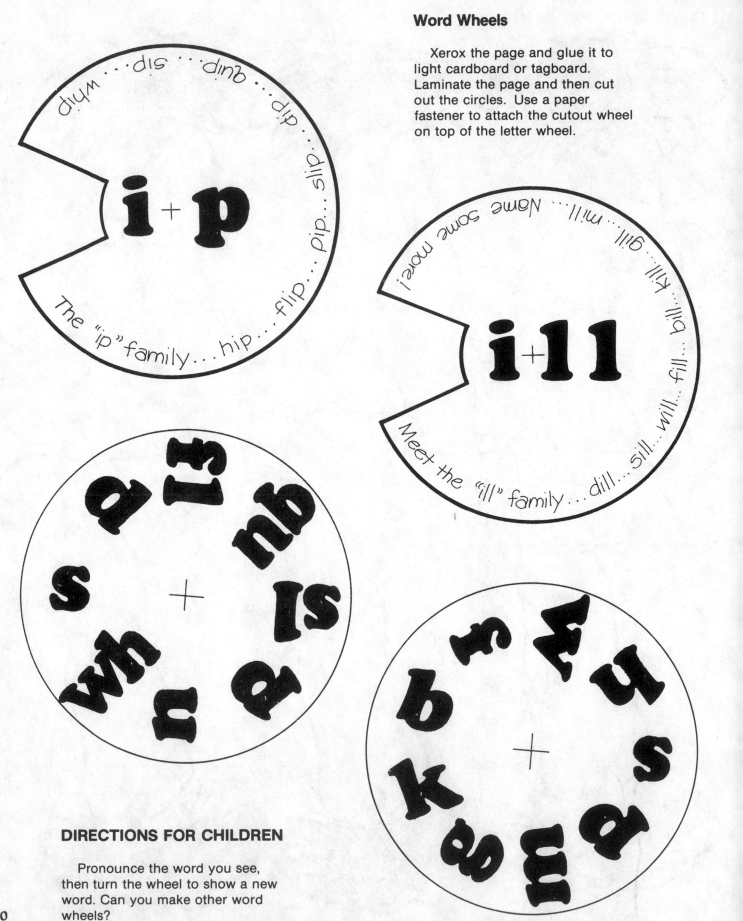

whip...sip...quip...dip...slip...pip...flip...hip...The "ip" family

Name some more!...mill...gill...kill...fill...will...sill...dill...Meet the "ill" family

i + p

i + ll

DIRECTIONS FOR CHILDREN

Pronounce the word you see, then turn the wheel to show a new word. Can you make other word wheels?

150

From *Recipes for Learning* by Gail Lewis and Jean M. Shaw, ©1979 by Goodyear Publishing Company, Inc.

"Cut-Outs" for Concentration
(instructions are in the teacher's section, page 43.)

and

where

said

is

and

when

said

was

the

when

can

was

the

that

can

is

then

that

where

then

Number Sentences
(Directions appear on teacher's card, page 43.)

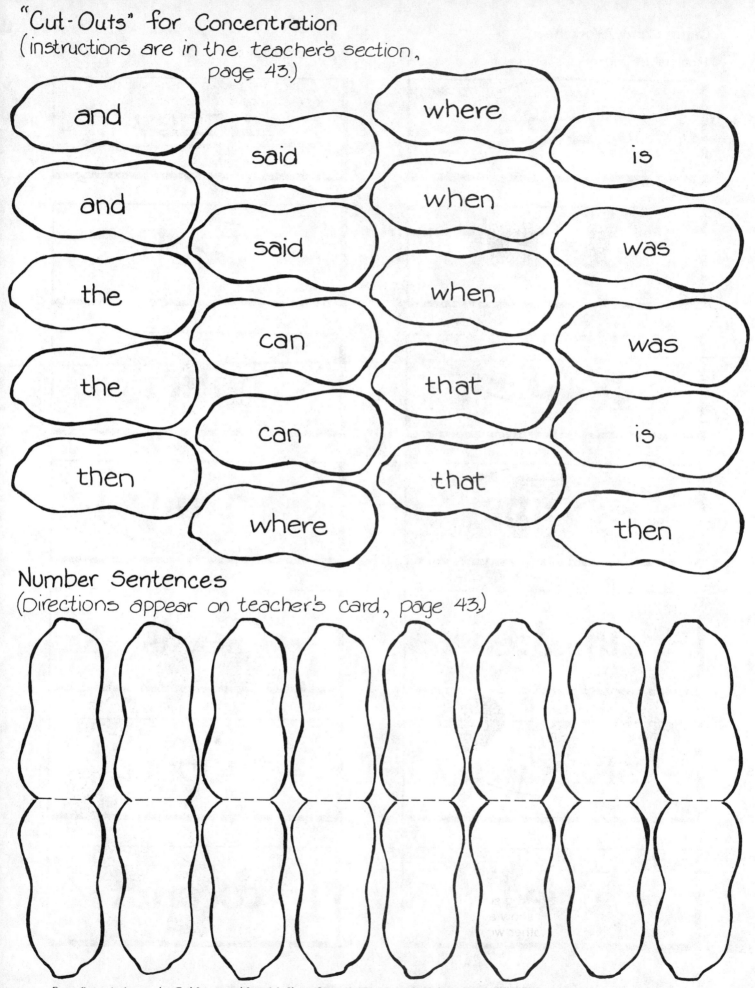

Carob Candy/Worksheet

Teacher: See suggestions for use on page 68.

cup	honey
peanut	carob
powder	butter
sesame	fruit
unsalted	seeds
shredded	chopped
dried	coconut

From *Recipes for Learning* by Gail Lewis and Jean M. Shaw, ©1979 by Goodyear Publishing Company, Inc.

Xerox the clown pages and glue the front to light cardboard or tagboard. Color both sides of the clown several different bright colors with crayons, markers, or paint. (Make sure there are several green dots and several yellow dots on both the front and back, along with other colors.) Laminate both front and back, or cover with clear contact paper. Cut out both sides and glue the front to the back. Cut the V-shaped slits on the hands so that balls can be inserted in them.

GRAY

BLACK

ORANGE

PURPLE

YELLOW

WHITE

PINK

BLUE

GREEN

RED

fold

fold

Balls for Use with Color Clown

Xerox these pages and glue them to light cardboard or tagboard. Color the balls in different colors, or leave some of them plain for coloring activities. Laminate the pages or cover them with clear contact paper, and then cut out the balls (there is no need to paste backs to fronts).

After they are laminated you may write whatever words or problems you wish on the blank balls; they may be wiped clean with wet or dry tissues or paper towels when you want to reuse them.

154

Pancakes

Xerox these pages. Cut and fold the envelope and staple the edges. Glue the "pancake" pages to tagboard or light cardboard and cut out the pancakes.

Have the children draw numbered pancakes out of the envelope to see who adds which pancake ingredient as you follow the recipe.

To use the other pancakes, have each child draw one out of the envelope and do the "mini-assignment" given on that pancake.

From *Recipes for Learning* by Gail Lewis and Jean M. Shaw, ©1979 by Goodyear Publishing Company, Inc.

fold →

fold ↑

Make pancakes at home to surprise your family.

Make a list of all the kinds of **CAKES** you can think of.

Read Hundreds of Pancakes by Audrey Chalmers.

Use the letters in **PANCAKE** and make as many new words as you can.

Cut out pancake shapes. Make creatures or designs from the shapes.

Read more about **crepes** — the French pancake.

Find out about **Pancake Day**.

Make a list of all the things that could be eaten **on** pancakes.

Read the "Mix a Pancake" poem by Christina Rossetti.

Read about **tortillas** — the Mexican corn pancake.

Read Round is a Pancake by Joan Sullivan in Sounds Around the Clock.

Read Journey Cake, Ho! by Robert McCloskey.

Read The Pancake, retold by George Webbe Dasent, Childcraft, Vol.2: Stories and Fables.

Tell the story of "The Runaway Pancake" to some friends. Use flannelboard characters.

156

From *Recipes for Learning* by Gail Lewis and Jean M. Shaw, ©1979 by Goodyear Publishing Company, Inc.

fractions

Teacher: see directions for "fractions" on page 88.

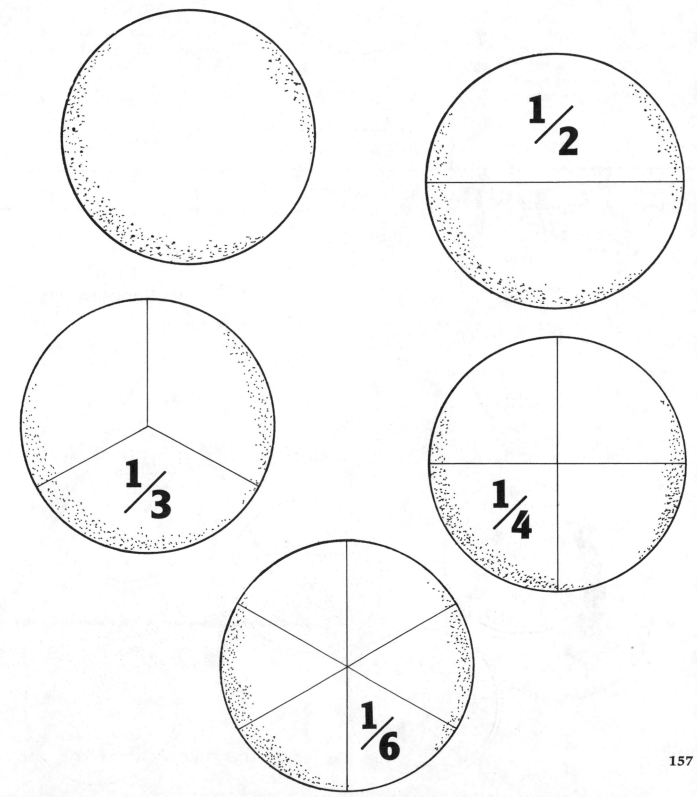

Play Dough Cards

Xerox the play dough cards pages and glue them to tagboard or light cardboard. Color the drawings if you wish. Laminate the pages or cover them with clear contact paper and then cut the cards apart.

Have the children mold dough over each shape, and use letter cards to make words.

Use light cardboard or tagboard to make more cards, and let the children trade cards.

Happy Modeling!

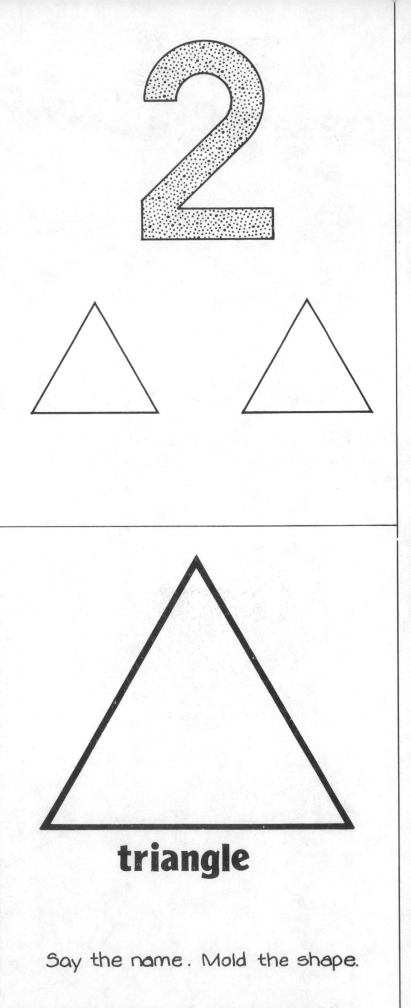

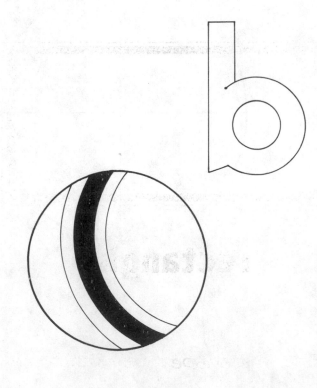

triangle

Say the name. Mold the shape.

158

3×4

Mold each dot in the array.
Count them.

2+3

Mold the numerals and the dots.
Count the answer.

cat

Mold the letters and the shape.

rectangle

Mold the shape. Say the name.

159

dog

d

tree

t

glove

g

pencil

p

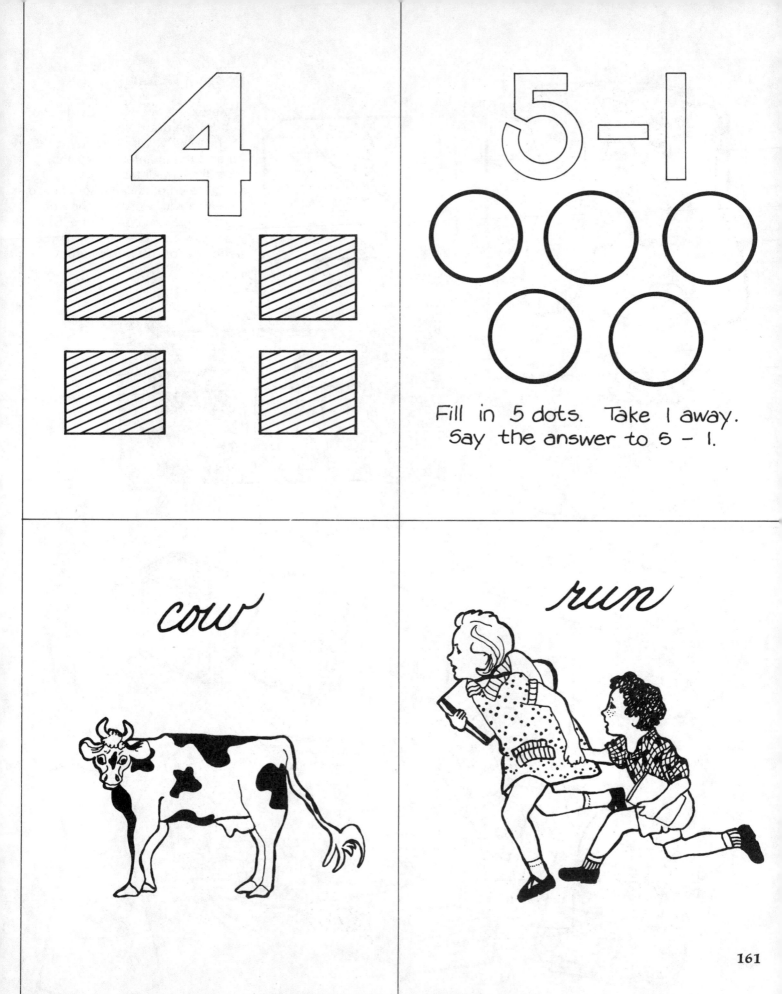

4

5-1

Fill in 5 dots. Take 1 away.
Say the answer to 5 - 1.

cow

run

Popcorn Cutouts

Xerox the popcorn cutouts and cut out the drawings.

Have the children name the objects the pictures show, and have them spell the words.

These cutouts can also be used to match with words on the Popcorn recipe, page 97. There are more ideas on the teacher card on page 101 for using this cutout page.

Vegetable Stew Cutouts

Xerox the pages of vegetable drawings and glue them to tagboard or light cardboard. Color or paint the vegetable pictures. Laminate the pages or cover them with clear contact paper. Cut out the vegetable pictures and the word cards.

THINGS TO DO:

- Match the word cards to the pictures.
- Classify the vegetables—have the children suggest such categories as
    color
    shape—long and thin or short and fat
    where they grow—above ground or below ground
    whether they are eaten raw, cooked, or both
    food values
- Use the vegetable pictures to make a mobile or bulletin board display.
- Use them for a matching game with Vege-Riddles, page 106.

lima beans

green beans

corn

carrot

cauliflower

tomato

onion

celery

potato

peas

yellow beans

beets

From *Recipes for Learning* by Gail Lewis and Jean M. Shaw, ©1979 by Goodyear Publishing Company, Inc.

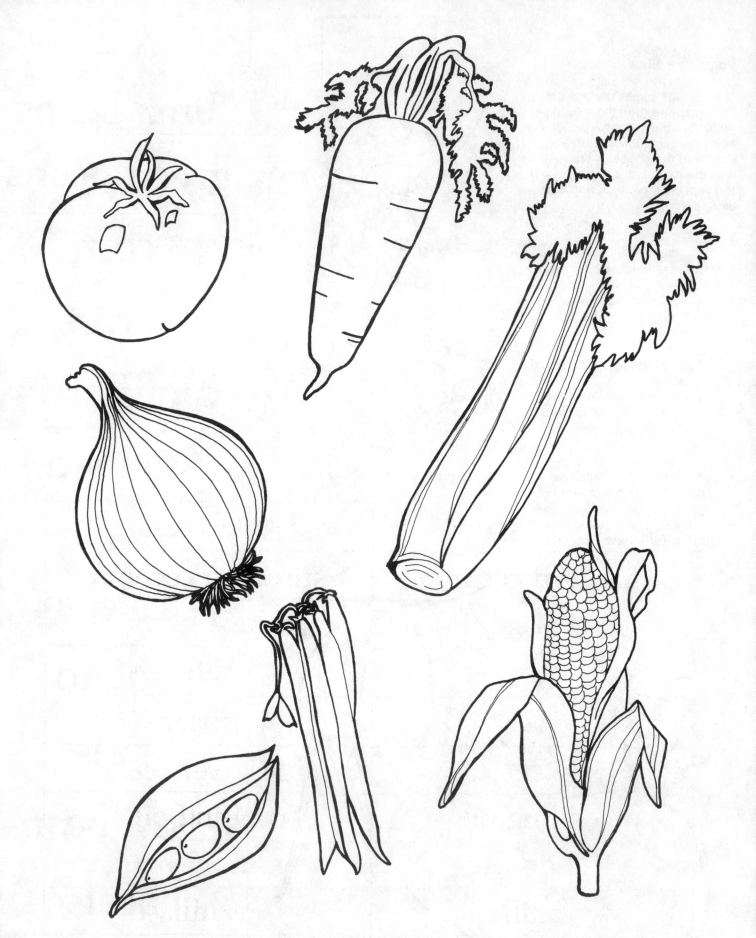

164

Granola Cutouts

Xerox the page of symbols and labels. Color the symbols to correspond to the colors used on the Granola recipe on page 117. Cut out the symbols and labels. Tape the symbols to the actual ingredients you use, for a color and shape-matching activity.

The ingredient labels may be attached to the actual containers, or they may be used in a matching activity with the real containers. They may also be used in an alphabetizing exercise.

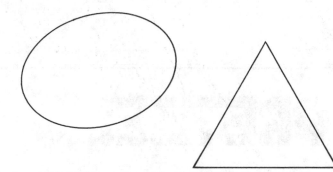

rolled oats	rolled oats
shredded coconut	shredded coconut
wheat germ	wheat germ
nuts	nuts
soybeans	soybeans
sunflower seeds	sunflower seeds
cooking oil	cooking oil
honey	honey
vanilla	vanilla
salt	salt

165

Box ↓

PICK A PRETZEL
GAME

Xerox the pages of pretzels and glue the fronts to tagboard or light cardboard. Color the box and the pretzels. Laminate them or cover them with clear contact paper. Cut out the pretzel letters and numbers, and glue the fronts and backs together. Glue the box onto a cereal box, shoe box, or sack.

Have the students take turns pulling out letters and naming them. Or, play the "direction game" by doing the actions indicated on the backs of the letters.

To use the numbers, put them in the pretzel box. Have the students pull out two numerals and tell which is larger, or have them add, subtract or multiply the two numbers.

From *Recipes for Learning* by Gail Lewis and Jean M. Shaw, ©1979 by Goodyear Publishing Company, Inc.

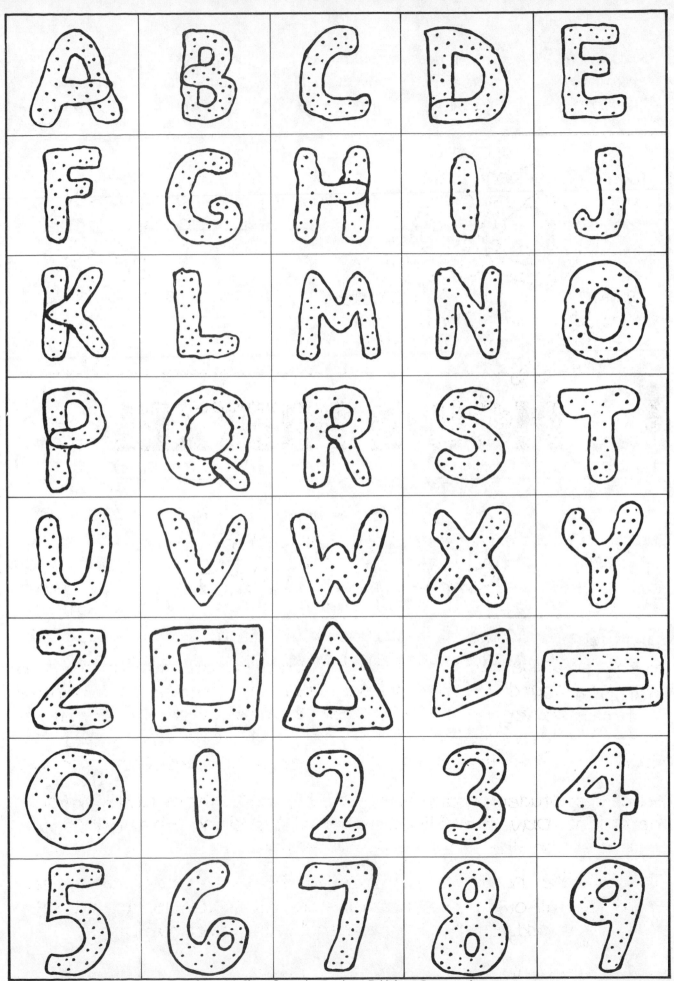

From *Recipes for Learning* by Gail Lewis and Jean M. Shaw, ©1979 by Goodyear Publishing Company, Inc.

Rub your tummy 4 times	Run in place 10 times.	Roll your eyes up— stand up.	Walk 2 steps backwards then 1 forward.	Turn around 3 times.
Take 2 jumps, then 1 hop.	Tap your head, then touch your toes once.	Do 3 sit ups.	Point to the ceiling then to your toes.	Blink your eyes 4 times.
Stamp your feet 8 times.	Clap 6 times.	Touch your right ear, then your left. Touch your nose.	Touch your toes 2 times.	Touch your hair, then your ears.
Blink your eyes 2 times then touch your head.	"Skate" around the floor, then sit down.	Hop on 1 foot 5 times.	Make a silly face, then frown.	Raise your eyebrows 3 times, then stand up.
Tap your right foot, then, your left foot.	Shrug your shoulders 4 times.	Clap 5 times very loud, then clap quietly 5 times.	Make a scary face, then smile.	Walk forward 4 steps, then backward 3 steps.
Hop 4 times, then jump 4 times.	Make a sad face, then blink your eyes 3 times.	Raise your eyebrows, then jump 2 times.	Run in place 16 times. Then sit down and rest.	Trace a circle in the air, then a triangle.
				Do 4 situps, then sit down.

From *Recipes for Learning* by Gail Lewis and Jean M. Shaw, ©1979 by Goodyear Publishing Company, Inc.

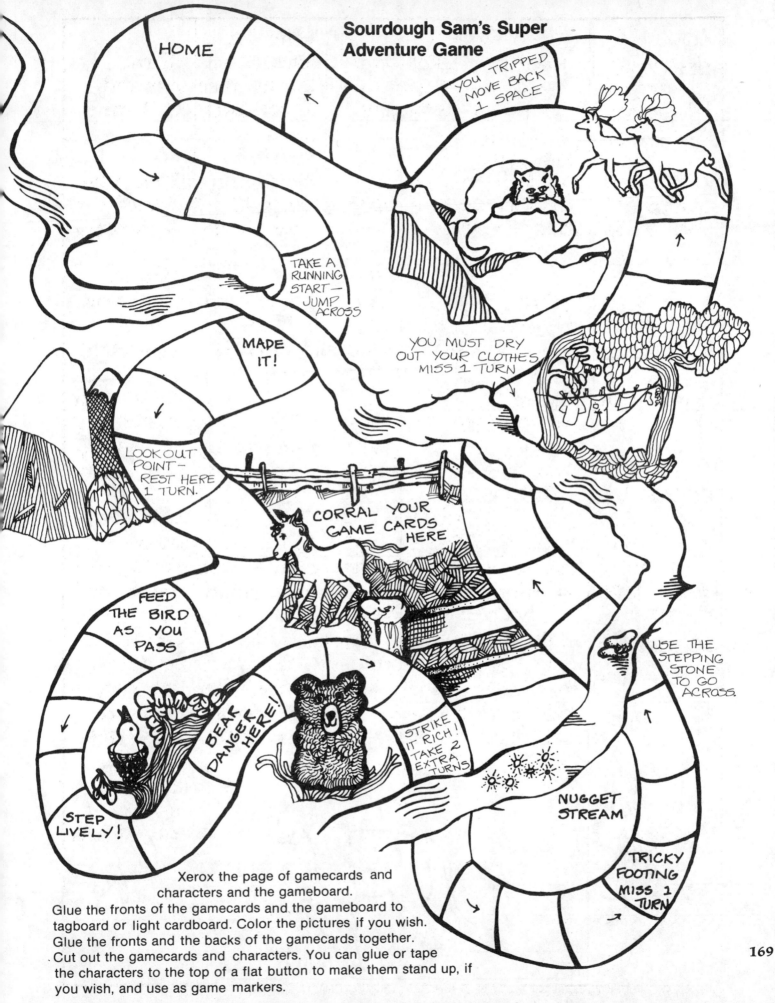

Sourdough Sam's Super Adventure Game

HOME

YOU TRIPPED MOVE BACK 1 SPACE

TAKE A RUNNING START— JUMP ACROSS

YOU MUST DRY OUT YOUR CLOTHES MISS 1 TURN

MADE IT!

LOOK OUT POINT— REST HERE 1 TURN.

CORRAL YOUR GAME CARDS HERE

FEED THE BIRD AS YOU PASS

USE THE STEPPING STONE TO GO ACROSS.

BEAR DANGER HERE!

STRIKE IT RICH! TAKE 2 EXTRA TURNS

NUGGET STREAM

STEP LIVELY!

TRICKY FOOTING MISS 1 TURN

Xerox the page of gamecards and characters and the gameboard.
Glue the fronts of the gamecards and the gameboard to tagboard or light cardboard. Color the pictures if you wish.
Glue the fronts and the backs of the gamecards together.
Cut out the gamecards and characters. You can glue or tape the characters to the top of a flat button to make them stand up, if you wish, and use as game markers.

169

From *Recipes for Learning* by Gail Lewis and Jean M. Shaw, ©1979 by Goodyear Publishing Company, Inc.

Move 1 space	Move 2 spaces	Move 3 spaces	HARD LUCK Move back 1 space
Move 1 space	Move 2 spaces	Move 3 spaces	HARD LUCK Move back 2 spaces
Move 1 space	Move 2 spaces	Move 3 spaces	BONUS 1 extra turn
Move 1 space	Move 2 spaces	BONUS 1 extra turn	BONUS 1 extra turn
Move 1 space	Move 1 space		

"SALLY"

"SUZY"

glue

glue

GLUE OR TAPE ENDS TOGETHER

"SMITHY"

"SAM"

From *Recipes for Learning* by Gail Lewis and Jean M. Shaw, ©1979 by Goodyear Publishing Company, Inc.

Classification Glasses

Cut pictures or words from old newspapers or magazines of things to drink. Choose which classification you would like to do (1, 2, 3 or 4). Now, classify and paste your pictures or words in the glasses.
[See teacher card, page 32.]

Write at least one rhyming word for each fruit name.

APPLE_____   FIG_____

PEAR _____   LIME_____

PEACH _____   CHERRY_____

DATE _____   GRAPE_____

171

My name is _____

Sequence Salad

Cut the cards out and arrange in the correct sequence for a recipe. Paste on a piece of paper in the correct order. You may wish to try making this recipe at home or at school.

| Cut in half. | Spread peanut butter. | Remove seeds and core. |
| Make a face with marshmallows and raisins. | Wash apple. | EAT ! |

172

From *Recipes for Learning* by Gail Lewis and Jean M. Shaw, ©1979 by Goodyear Publishing Company, Inc.

Complete the Patterns

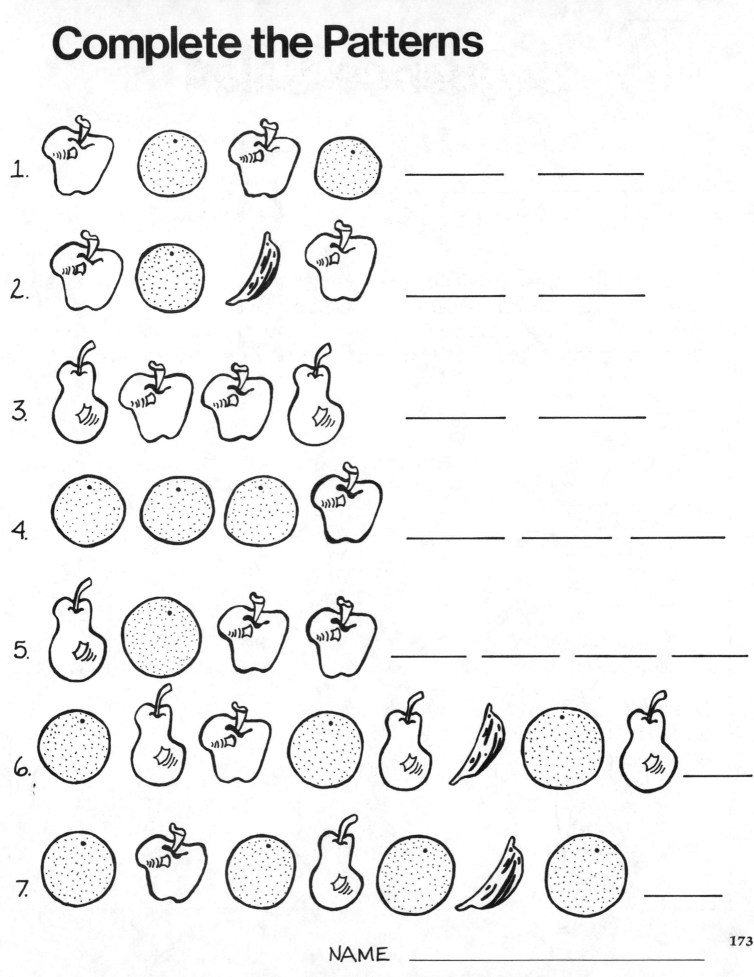

1. _____ _____

2. _____ _____

3. _____ _____

4. _____ _____ _____ _____

5. _____ _____ _____

6. _____

7. _____

NAME _____

From *Recipes for Learning* by Gail Lewis and Jean M. Shaw, ©1979 by Goodyear Publishing Company, Inc.

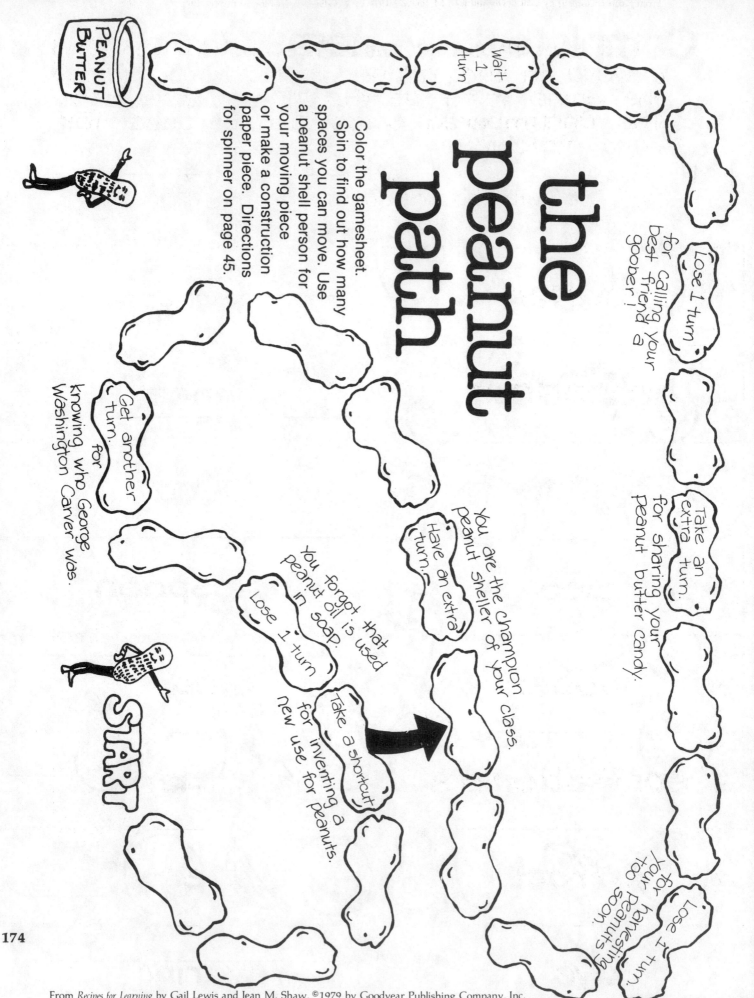

the peanut path

Color the gamesheet. Spin to find out how many spaces you can move. Use a peanut shell person for your moving piece or make a construction paper piece. Directions for spinner on page 45.

PEANUT BUTTER

Wait 1 turn

for calling your best friend a goober!

Lose 1 turn

Take an extra turn.

for sharing your peanut butter candy.

Lose 1 turn for your harvesting too soon.

You are the champion peanut sheller of your class.

Have an extra turn.

You forgot that peanut oil is used in soap.

Lose 1 turn for inventing a new use for peanuts.

Take a shortcut

Get another turn.

for knowing who George Washington Carver was.

START

174

From *Recipes for Learning* by Gail Lewis and Jean M. Shaw, ©1979 by Goodyear Publishing Company, Inc.

Cut out these words. See if you can find a word in the recipe that means almost the same thing as the numbered cards. The unnumbered cards can be used for word matching.

Use with the standard or metric recipe for Peanut Butter Candy pages 41 and 42.

1.	butter	Blend
2.	groundnut	ounce
3.	pindas	pound
4.	oleo	Tablespoon
5.	goober	food
6.	confectioners	together
7.	extract	butter
8.	dye	flavoring

CUT-OUT NUMBER CARDS
POPCORN WORKSHEET

Cut out number cards.
Cut on the solid lines and fold on the dotted lines. "Fill" each bowl by drawing the correct number of popped or unpopped corn printed inside each bowl. Check the way you have filled each bowl by looking at the dots under the fold.

From *Recipes for Learning* by Gail Lewis and Jean M. Shaw, ©1979 by Goodyear Publishing Company, Inc.

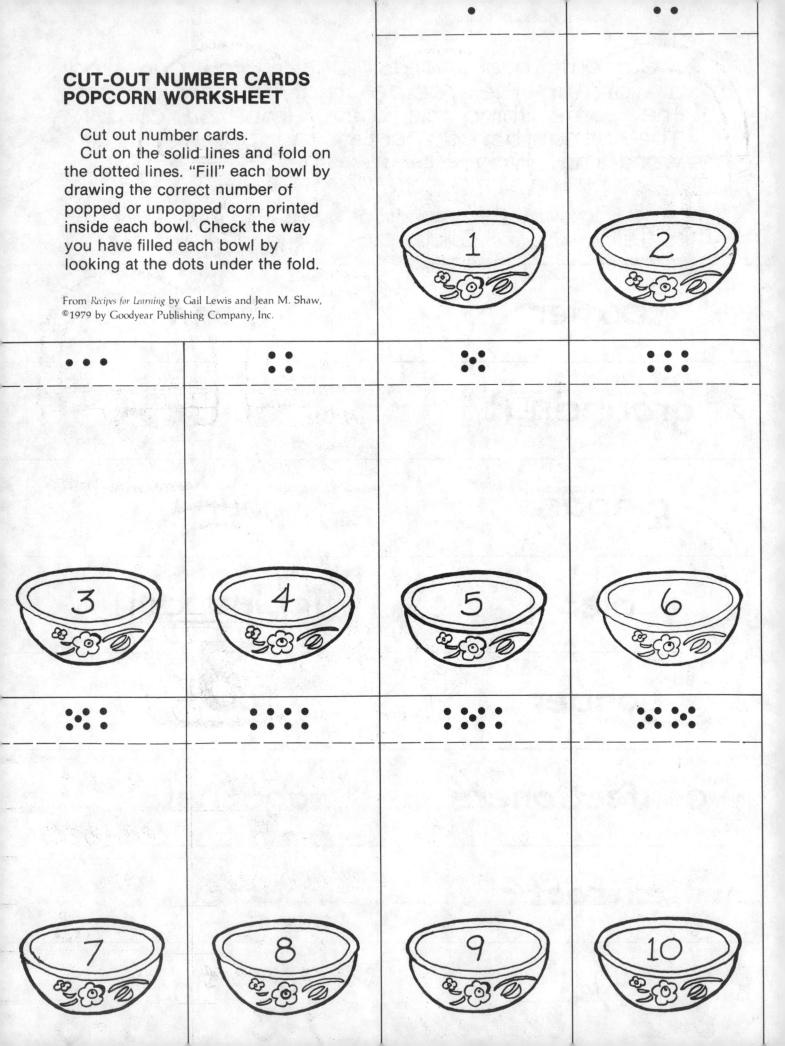

From *Recipes for Learning* by Gail Lewis and Jean M. Shaw, ©1979 by Goodyear Publishing Company, Inc.

Cut out these cards and put them in the basket with the correct answer. 🍎	7+2	🍎🍎🍎 + 🍎🍎🍎	9 + 1
	🍎🍎 + 🍎🍎	5 + 5	🍎🍎 + 🍎🍎🍎
5 +2	2 +4	🍎🍎🍎🍎🍎 + 🍎🍎🍎	🍎🍎 + 🍎
3 + 0	3 + 1	3 + 5	6 + 3
🍎🍎🍎🍎 + 🍎🍎🍎	6 + 1	🍎🍎🍎🍎🍎🍎 + 🍎🍎🍎	4 + 1
6 + 2	🍎🍎🍎 + 🍎🍎🍎	7 + 3	1 + 5

What Do I Weigh?

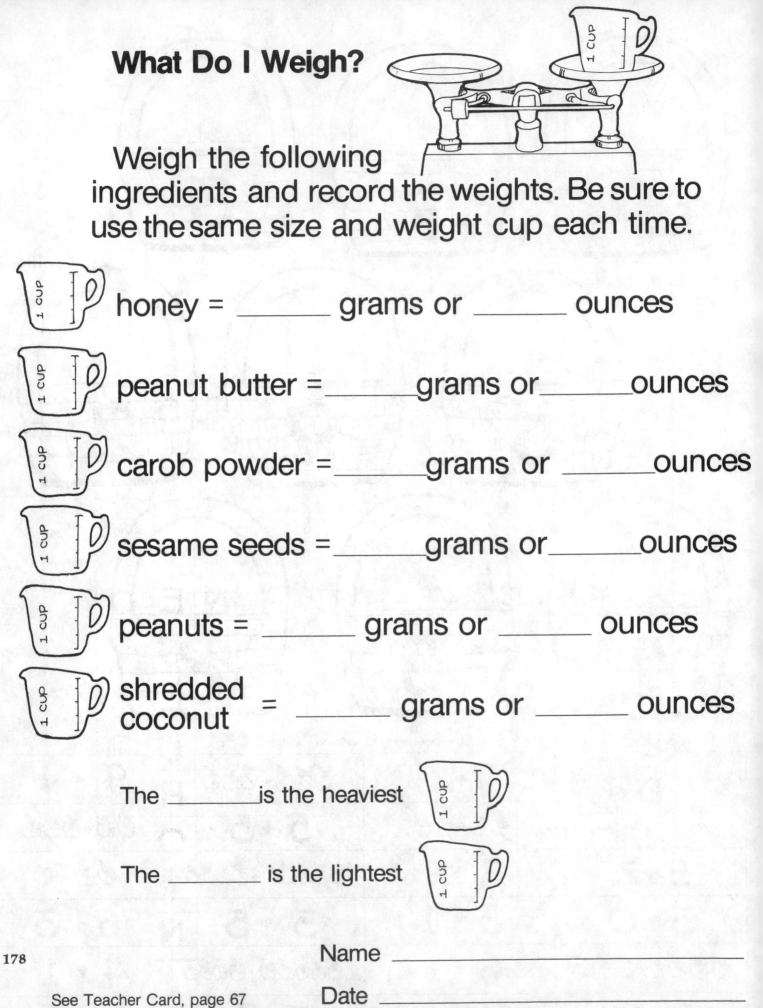

Weigh the following ingredients and record the weights. Be sure to use the same size and weight cup each time.

honey = _____ grams or _____ ounces

peanut butter = _____ grams or _____ ounces

carob powder = _____ grams or _____ ounces

sesame seeds = _____ grams or _____ ounces

peanuts = _____ grams or _____ ounces

shredded coconut = _____ grams or _____ ounces

The _____ is the heaviest

The _____ is the lightest

Name _____

Date _____

See Teacher Card, page 67

From *Recipes for Learning* by Gail Lewis and Jean M. Shaw, ©1979 by Goodyear Publishing Company, Inc.

Word Hunt

Find the words below in the maze. Cross out each one as you find it.
One word is circled for you.

cold	jello	pan
cup	gelatin	stir
cut	heat	soften
dissolve	milliliter	hot
finger	measure	water

(Use with Finger Jell-O recipe, pages 73-74)

A	E	L	Q	Z	A	W	B	I	F	S	H
C	R	M	X	M	J	D	Y	D	I	O	G
S	F	I	N	G	E	R	H	C	P	F	J
B	F	L	B	M	L	E	K	D	A	T	K
G	T	L	G	E	L	A	T	I	N	E	O
C	K	I	H	A	O	C	F	S	D	N	P
O	U	L	V	S	N	G	M	S	L	E	T
L	I	I	P	U	A	N	O	O	C	U	P
D	S	T	I	R	C	H	C	L	S	H	W
J	Q	E	R	E	E	E	U	V	X	O	Y
K	G	R	D	F	W	A	T	E	R	T	Z
W	L	Y	I	B	O	T	M	H	J	N	P

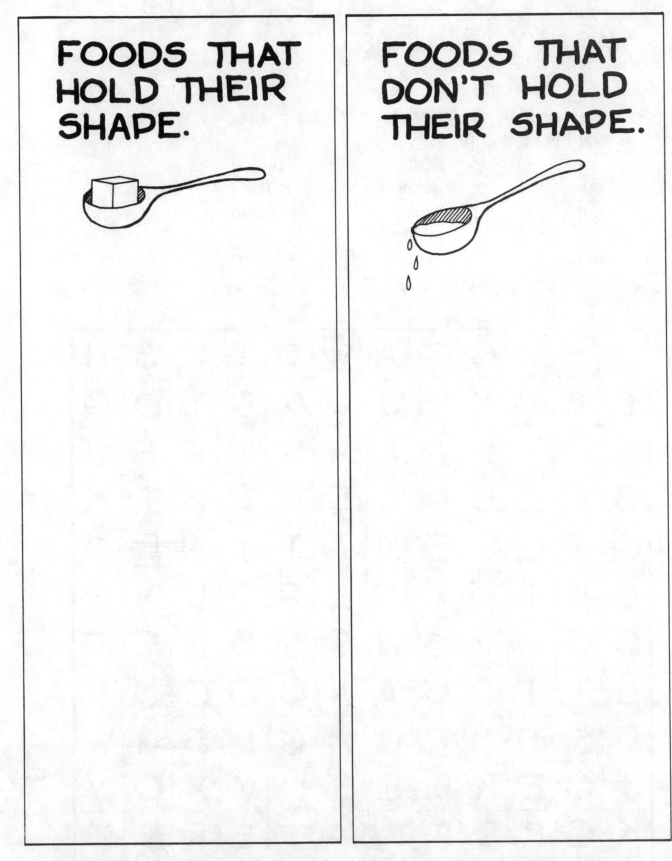

FOODS THAT HOLD THEIR SHAPE.

FOODS THAT DON'T HOLD THEIR SHAPE.

While you wait for gelatin to soften, talk about foods that hold their shape and those that don't. Write a list for each type. Children can work together or alone. Pictures can be used rather than words. The children can sort these into the two categories.

180

From *Recipes for Learning* by Gail Lewis and Jean M. Shaw, ©1979 by Goodyear Publishing Company, Inc.

COLORS EVERYWHERE!

Read the poem. Color in the boxes around the color words. Color the pictures. Read your colorful poem again!

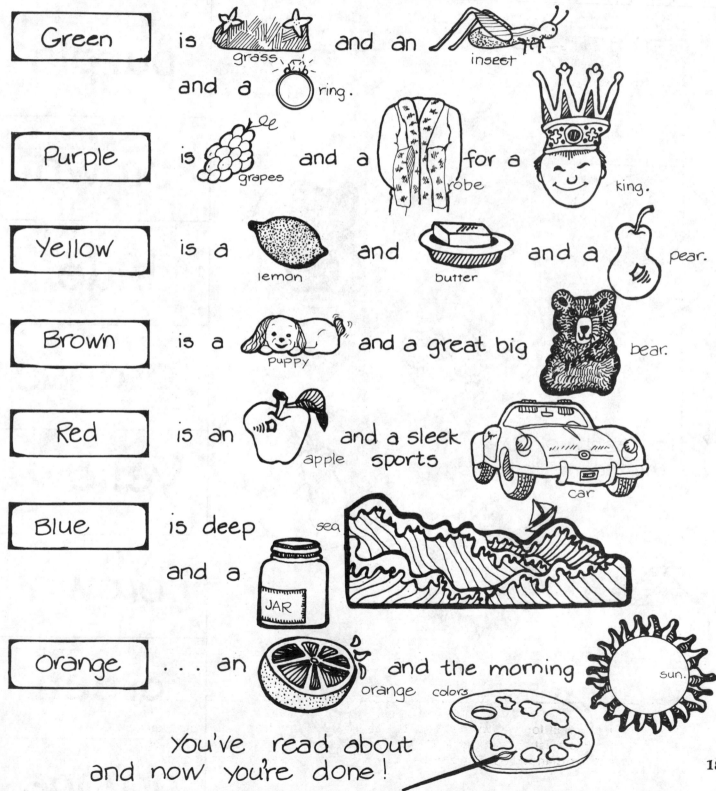

Green is grass and an insect and a ring.

Purple is grapes and a robe for a king.

Yellow is a lemon and butter and a pear.

Brown is a puppy and a great big bear.

Red is an apple and a sleek sports car.

Blue is deep sea and a JAR

Orange ... an orange and the morning colors sun.

You've read about and now you're done!

181

From *Recipes for Learning* by Gail Lewis and Jean M. Shaw, ©1979 by Goodyear Publishing Company, Inc.

Color Fun

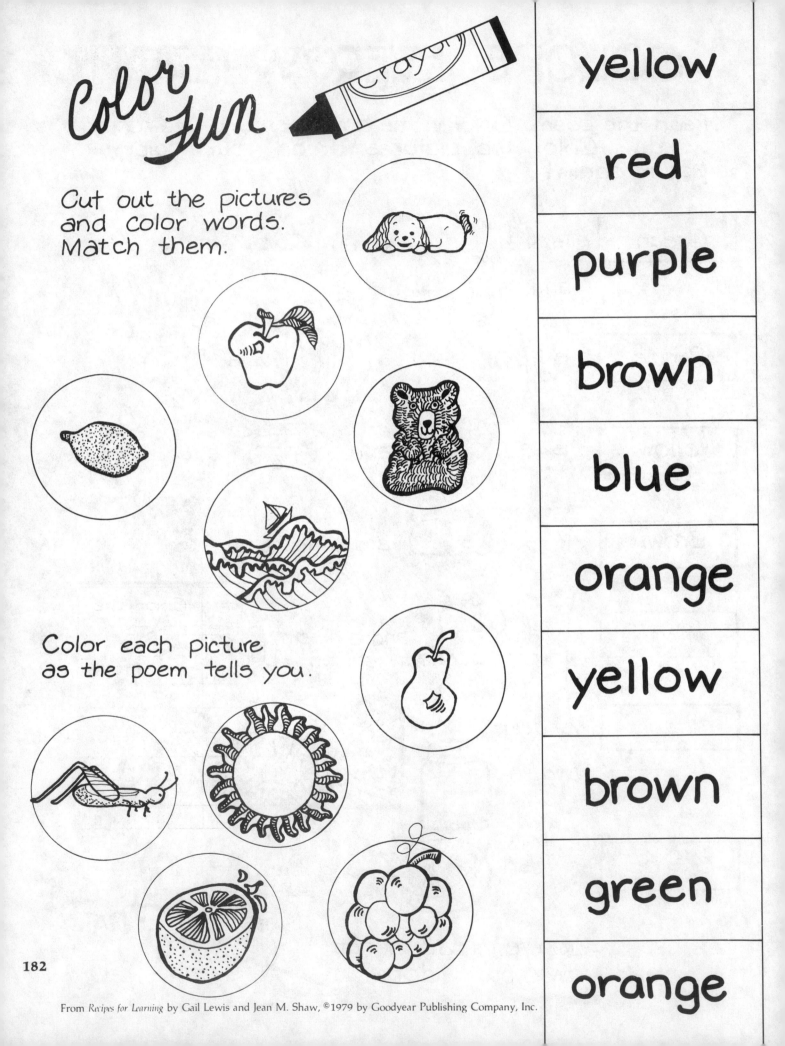

Cut out the pictures
and color words.
Match them.

Color each picture
as the poem tells you.

yellow

red

purple

brown

blue

orange

yellow

brown

green

orange

182

From *Recipes for Learning* by Gail Lewis and Jean M. Shaw, ©1979 by Goodyear Publishing Company, Inc.

COLOR MATH CLOWN

If the answer is:	Color the space
1	red
2	orange
3	yellow
4	green
5	blue
6	purple
7	brown
8	black

From *Recipes for Learning* by Gail Lewis and Jean M. Shaw, ©1979 by Goodyear Publishing Company, Inc.

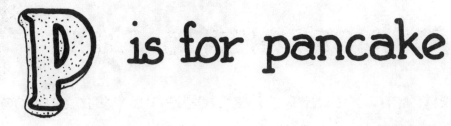 **is for pancake**

How many foods can you list that begin with "P"?

_____   _____

_____   _____

_____   _____

_____   _____

_____   _____

How many other words can you list that begin with "P"?

_____   _____

_____   _____

_____   _____

_____   _____

_____   _____

Name: _____

Date: _____

MYSTERY INGREDIENTS GAME

Use this chart with the jars of ingredients your teacher has for you. Record your guess under each jar number using only the sense(s) listed to the left. Check your last guesses with the answer card provided by your teacher.

	JAR 1	JAR 2	JAR 3	JAR 4	JAR 5
SIGHT					
SIGHT & SOUND					
SIGHT, SOUND & SMELL					
SIGHT, SOUND, SMELL & TOUCH					
SIGHT, SOUND, SMELL, TOUCH & TASTE					

Teacher: See directions p. 88

Name _____

Date _____

185

From *Recipes for Learning* by Gail Lewis and Jean M. Shaw, ©1979 by Goodyear Publishing Company, Inc.

Area Estimation

Estimate how many kernels of corn will go in each shape. Write down your estimation. Then count how many kernels it really took to fill in the area of each shape.

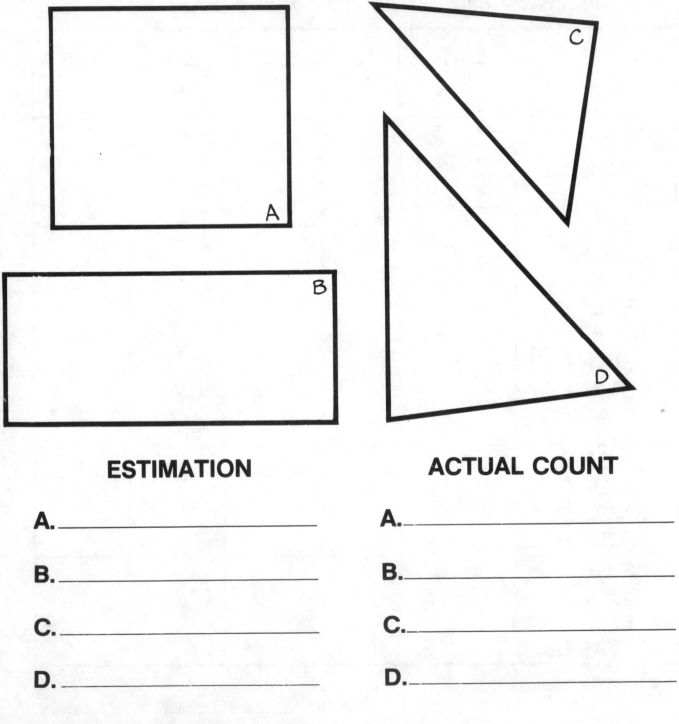

ESTIMATION	ACTUAL COUNT
A._____	A._____
B._____	B._____
C._____	C._____
D._____	D._____

Teacher: See Area Estimation p. 101.

From *Recipes for Learning* by Gail Lewis and Jean M. Shaw, ©1979 by Goodyear Publishing Company, Inc.

Finish a Story...

If I were a kernel of popcorn_____

_____

_____

_____

_____

_____

_____

_____

_____

_____

_____

_____

_____

_____

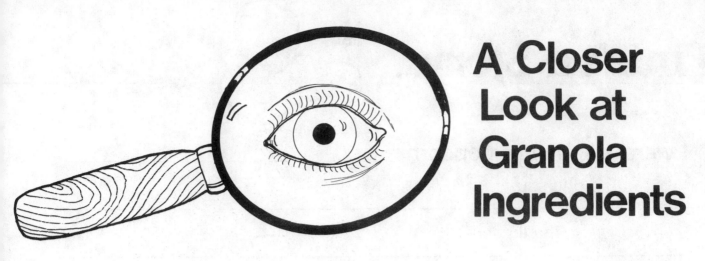

A Closer Look at Granola Ingredients

Pick out 6 granola ingredients and put them in 3 pairs. Now look closely at the pairs of ingredients to find ways they are alike and ways they are different.

1. Ingredients: _____ _____
   They are alike because _____

   _____
   They are different because _____

   _____

2. Ingredients: _____ _____
   They are alike because _____

   _____
   They are different because _____

   _____

3. Ingredients: _____ _____
   They are alike because _____

   _____
   They are different because _____

   _____

188

Simple Food Tests

Test for Fat

1. Cut some brown paper squares.
2. Rub food on one square of paper.
3. Let it dry.
4. If fat is present, the light will show through.

Test for Starch

1. Get some tincture of iodine from the drug store.
2. Put a drop of iodine on the food you want to test. *Handle with care —* IODINE IS POISON!!
3. If starch is present the iodine will turn dark blue or black.

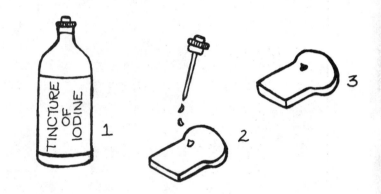

Test for Protein

1. Obtain some potassium hydroxide or sodium hydroxide. You can get these from a chemistry set, a science teacher, or the drug store. Also obtain some copper sulfate. You can make a solution of this from crystals from the drug store.
2. Add the food you want to test to a sodium or potassium hydroxide solution.
3. Add a few drops of copper sulfate.
4. If protein is present, you will see a pinkish or bluish color.

189

From *Recipes for Learning* by Gail Lewis and Jean M. Shaw, ©1979 by Goodyear Publishing Company, Inc.

Food Tests and Food Values

Perform the food tests on 8 foods. Look up information on the foods.   Record the results here.

(this sheet may be used for any recipe with 8 or more ingredients)

| Food | Information from Food Tests | | | Information from Reference Materials Food Values |
	Fat	Starch	Protein	
1.				
2.				
3.				
4.				
5.				
6.				
7.				
8.				

190

Pretzel Space Man
and His Pets

Find all the letters and shapes you can. Color them.

191

From *Recipes for Learning* by Gail Lewis and Jean M. Shaw, ©1979 by Goodyear Publishing Company, Inc.

FIND-A-WORD MAZE

The words below are hidden in the maze. They may be found across, down, or diagonally. Circle them as you find them. You may find other words also.

pretzel	bake	divide	egg	paint
salt	mix	brush	yeast	measure
sugar	glaze	alphabet	shape	dough
water	bowl	word	knead	envelope

```
A P R E T Z E L K H S F A M
K B G D O U G H E D A L L O
D I R D O W N G Y I L M P R
J O B U O N E L N V T O H E
A F U C S U G A R I Y P A N
L D I G A H S Z Y D Q R B V
D S S V L S E E R E Z T E E
H E H T T W A N G O A I T L
A M E A S U R E H G Y S J O
B M I G P T O E B O W L T P
E F L X V E U W A T E R K E
T K N E A D P O K B R E A D
T E D F O U R R E A C R O S
E G G L W B X D A P A I N T
```

APPENDIX

Parent Involvement and Take-Home Metric Recipes

PARENT INVOLVEMENT

Using cooking in the classroom offers many opportunities to involve parents in their children's education. Some parents will have the time and desire to help you at school while others may be able to help in other ways. Following are some parent-involvement ideas.

Parents become helpers . . . through contributions—money, ingredients, equipment, utensils; through sharing time at school or by taking a small group shopping for ingredients; through sharing recipes and information—for example, an ethnic dish or helpful methods of food preparation.

Parents become friends . . . through an open house or parent-education meeting for which the children could prepare refreshments; through visits to school to watch children learning through cooking.

Parents become involved . . . through newsletters written by you and the children and sharing new words learned, activities related to cooking, etc.; through school recipes tried at home; through thank-you notes written by the children for their parents' help.

Parents become more aware . . . through using metric recipes at home with their children; through watching their children's enthusiasm and cognitive growth related to cooking; through your personal contact and concern for their children.

The following letter is an example of how you might introduce your cooking program to parents at the beginning of the year.

Dear Parent,

We will be cooking in our classroom this year. There are many benefits from a classroom cooking program. Children learn by experiencing. Cooking gives children an opportunity to measure, count, add, subtract, multiply, divide, and work with fractions in a meaningful way. New words and concepts are introduced as new foods are prepared. Children learn to cooperate and refine social skills as well as to practice health and safety procedures. We will be preparing foods that not only taste good but are nutritious.

Please check items below if you can help us in any way. If you have any questions, please let me know.

Sincerely,

Your child's teacher

SAMPLE ITEMS:

_____ 1. I would be willing to donate ingredients occasionally.

_____ 2. I would like to come to school one day to help.

_____ 3. I would be willing to donate the following utensils (list things).

Homemade Butter

Pour 250 ml whipping cream into a medium jar with tight-fitting lid. Add 3 ml salt and two drops yellow food coloring. Close jar tightly. SHAKE! Butter will form after several minutes. Pour off any liquid. Serve immediately or chill and serve later.

Carrot and Celery Snacks

454 g carrots
1 bunch celery

Carefully wash carrots. Scrape with vegetable peeler or edge of knife. Cut into strips, "coins", or bias bits.

Cut off end of celery bunch. Separate the stalks and wash them well. Cut into "c's", sticks, or fans. Put pieces in ice water. Chill. Drain before serving. Serve plain or with a dip.

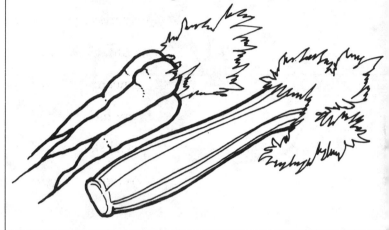

Peanut Butter Candy

100 g peanut butter
1 stick margarine
454 g powdered sugar
15 ml vanilla flavoring
food coloring

Blend together peanut butter, margarine, and sugar. Add vanilla. Roll with hands to make different shapes. Food coloring can be kneaded in if desired. This candy can be made into pumpkins, apples, wreaths, or other seasonal shapes.

Dill Dip

500 ml mayonnaise
500 ml sour cream
45 ml dill weed
45 ml chopped onion
15 ml seasoned salt

Chop onion. Put mayonnaise, sour cream, dill, and salt in a bowl. Stir well. Use as a dip for chips, crackers, or fresh vegetables.

195

From *Recipes for Learning* by Gail Lewis and Jean M. Shaw, ©1979 by Goodyear Publishing Company, Inc.

Soap Sculpture

175 ml Ivory Snow
15 ml water

Mix with a hand beater or electric mixer until stiff. Let it dry overnight. Make any sculpture you like.

Apple Sauce

4-5 apples
½ stick cinnamon
125 ml water
125 ml sugar
3 ml nutmeg

Core, peel, and quarter apples. Boil in water with cinnamon 15-25 minutes. Add sugar and nutmeg. Mix well. Mash apples using hand beater or potato masher.

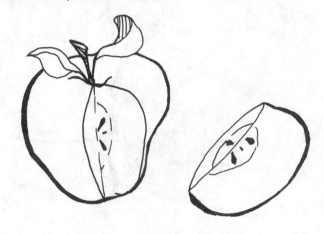

Carob Candy

250 ml honey
250 ml peanut butter
250 ml carob powder
250 ml sesame seeds
250 ml unsalted peanuts
125 ml shredded coconut
125 ml chopped dried fruit

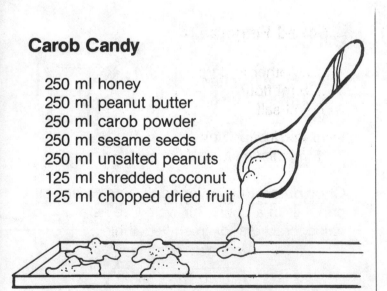

Heat honey and peanut butter until they can be mixed easily together. Quickly add carob powder and other ingredients and mix. Drop by spoonfuls onto waxed paper. Refrigerate until ready to eat. YUM!

196

Finger Jell-O

4 pkgs. unflavored gelatin
500 ml hot water
2 small pkgs. flavored gelatin
500 ml cold water

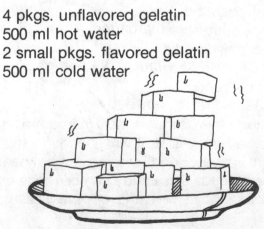

Stir unflavored gelatin into 100 ml hot water. Let soften about 15 minutes. Add flavored gelatin and 400 ml hot water. Stir until well dissolved. Add cold water. Very lightly grease a 22 x 30 cm pan. Pour gelatin in.

Refrigerate. When firm, cut into shapes. Eat with fingers.

From *Recipes for Learning* by Gail Lewis and Jean M. Shaw, ©1979 by Goodyear Publishing Company, Inc.

Popcorn

You will need: popcorn
                      vegetable oil
                      salt
                      popper or pan with lid

Pour enough oil to cover bottom of popper or pan. Put two kernels of corn in oil and cover popper with lid. When the kernels pop, the oil is hot enough to add the rest of the corn. (175 ml of popcorn kernels will make 2 liters of popped corn.)

Play Dough

250 ml flour
250 ml water
125 ml salt
10 ml cream of tartar
30 ml salad oil
Food coloring

Mix dry ingredients. Add oil and water. Cook 3 minutes or until mixture pulls away from sides of pan. Take the mixture out and, on a surface covered with waxed paper, knead in food coloring when dough is cool enough to touch.

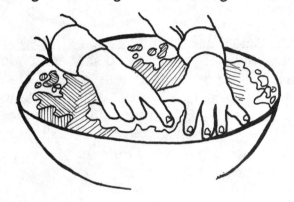

Pancakes

1. 250 ml milk
2. 30 ml melted margarine
3. 1 egg
4. 250 ml sifted flour
5. 30 ml sugar
6. 10 ml baking powder
7. 3 ml salt

Pour 1, 2, and 3 into a large bowl. Beat lightly. Add 4, 5, 6, and 7. Stir all ingredients together. Lightly grease skillet and heat it over medium heat. Pour batter into pan to make the size pancakes you want. Turn when bubbles form on top.

Cooked Fingerpaint

Stir together in pan:
    250 ml flour
    60 ml salt

Add gradually:
    1250 ml water

Cook over medium heat until thick. Add a small amount of powdered tempera paint. Use when cool. Store in refrigerator if kept more than two or three days. FUN!

197

From *Recipes for Learning* by Gail Lewis and Jean M. Shaw, ©1979 by Goodyear Publishing Company, Inc.

Vegetable Stew

Cooked soup bones
Many varieties of vegetables
1 pkg. onion-soup mix
Salt

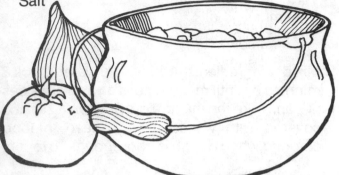

Wash vegetables carefully and cut into pieces. Make a variety of sizes and shapes—chunks, bias-cut strips, sticks, and others. Decide which vegetables must be cooked the longest (potatoes, beets, carrots) and put these in first. Add soup mix. Cook. After half an hour add other vegetables and cook until tender. Add more salt if needed.

Jell-O Popcorn Balls

1 stick margarine
500 ml miniature marshmallows
1 small pkg. flavored gelatin
4 liters popped corn

Pop corn. Set aside unsalted. Melt margarine in a medium pan. Add marshmallows and stir until melted. Add gelatin and stir until mixed. Pour over popped corn. Toss until mixed well. Form into balls with buttered hands.

Apple Popcorn

Pop 375 ml popcorn. This will make about 4 liters. Set aside in a large bowl. Melt 125 ml margarine in a saucepan. Add 250 ml dried apples, 125 ml brown sugar, and 5 ml apple spice, cinnamon, or pumpkin pie spice. Cook until apples are "puffy" and are beginning to brown. Pour mixture carefully over popped corn. Toss corn until it is evenly coated with mixture. SUPER GOOD!

Cheesy Corn

Mix: 250 ml grated cheese
125 ml melted oleo

Pour: over 4 liters popped corn

Toss: until popcorn and cheese mixture is mixed.

Add: salt to taste

198

From *Recipes for Learning* by Gail Lewis and Jean M. Shaw, ©1979 by Goodyear Publishing Company, Inc.

Alphabet Pretzels

Dissolve in a large bowl:
    125 ml water
    1 pkg. (7g) yeast

Mix in:
    1000 ml flour
    15 ml sugar

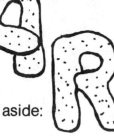

Beat in a small bowl and set aside:
    1 egg
    5 ml water

Mix yeast mixture with 750 ml of the flour-sugar mixture. Knead mixture and work in 250 ml flour. Divide dough into 20 to 30 pieces. Shape into letter forms. Paint with egg mixture. Sprinkle with salt. Bake at 450° F. (225° C) for 25 minutes.

"Crunchy" Granola

Mix together in large bowl:
    750 ml rolled oats
    250 ml shredded coconut
    175 ml wheat germ
    175 ml chopped nuts
    175 ml soybeans
    125 ml sunflower seeds
    75 ml cooking oil
    75 ml honey
    3 ml each of vanilla and salt

Bake in flat pan at 300° F. (150° C) until crisp and crunchy. Stir often. Serve as a nourishing snack.

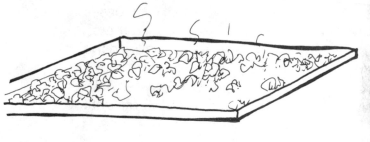

Sourdough Bread

    1 pkg. (7 g) dry yeast
    375 ml warm water
    250 ml sourdough starter
    15 ml salt
    15 ml sugar
    1375 to 1500 ml flour
    5 ml baking soda

In large bowl, soften yeast in warm water. Blend in starter, salt, and sugar. Add 625 ml flour. Blend well for 5 or 6 minutes. Cover; let rise until bubbly—about 1½ hours. Combine soda with 625 ml flour and stir into dough. Add enough additional flour to make a stiff dough. Turn out onto lightly floured board. Knead for 5 to 7 minutes. Place on greased baking sheet after forming into two loaves. Cut slashes in top. Bake at 400° F. (200° C) for 35-40 minutes.

Sourdough Starter

    1 pkg. (7 g) dry yeast
    625 ml warm water
    500 ml flour
    20 ml sugar

Dissolve yeast in 250 ml water. Stir in remaining water, flour, and sugar. Beat until smooth. Cover with cheesecloth, paper toweling, or plastic wrap. Let stand at room temperature five to ten days. Stir two or three times a day. (The time needed for the mixture to ferment will depend on room temperature. If the room is warm, let the mixture stand for a shorter time than if the room is cool.) Cover and refrigerate until ready for use. To keep starter going, add 200 ml flour, 200 ml water, and 10 ml sugar. Let stand at room temperature at least one day. Cover and refrigerate until ready to use.

199

From *Recipes for Learning* by Gail Lewis and Jean M. Shaw, ©1979 by Goodyear Publishing Company, Inc.